MW01260108

Especially for
From
Date

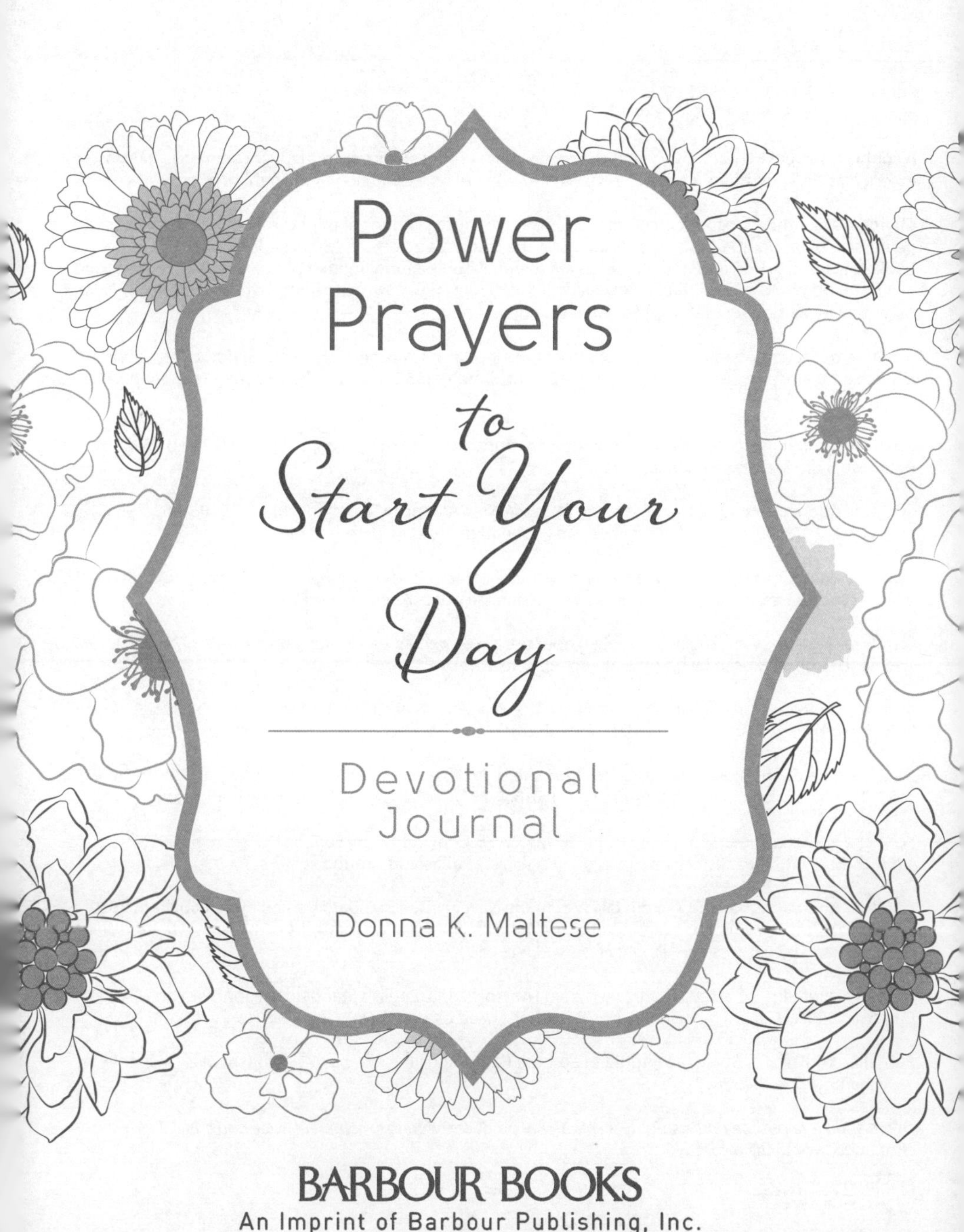

Power Prayers to Start Your Day

Devotional Journal

Donna K. Maltese

BARBOUR BOOKS
An Imprint of Barbour Publishing, Inc.

Print ISBN 978-1-63409-636-2
Special Edition ISBN 978-1-63409-852-6

Published by Barbour Books, an imprint of Barbour Publishing, Inc., P.O. Box 719, Uhrichsville, Ohio 44683, www.barbourbooks.com

Our mission is to publish and distribute inspirational products offering exceptional value and biblical encouragement to the masses.

Printed in China.

Introduction

Every new morning is spread before us like a blank canvas to paint as we choose. And the beginning of each new morning provides us with a choice as to who will be guiding our brush that day. Will it be our egocentric selves or our loving God? If we are wise, we will allow our hand to be directed by the Master Painter, the Ultimate Designer. He is our Creator, Companion, Protector, Confidant, and Friend, the One who can help us face whatever life may bring. Only in His power can we push away feelings of doubt, disappointment, dismay, and discouragement and fill our minds with hope, joy, peace, creativity, and a sense of expectancy. *Power Prayers to Start Your Day Devotional Journal* promises to aid in this early morning quest to seek God—for guidance, comfort, instruction, direction, strength, and love.

The Power of Stillness before God

This is what the Sovereign Lord, the Holy One of Israel, says. . .
"In quietness and trust is your strength."
Isaiah 30:15 niv

In this fast-paced, noisy world, quiet time is a precious commodity. If cell phones aren't ringing, the dog is barking or the kids are arguing. If the television isn't on, music is blaring nearby. If people aren't talking, your phone's alerts are dinging. That's why the early morning hours are ideal for quiet time before the Lord. The morning is your chance to spend time with God before the world fully awakens.

To ready your heart and mind for a meaningful time of prayer, adopt the three habits recommended by David Jeremiah. First, *anticipate* His presence. God is coming to see you, His sole desire to spend precious moments with you. Second, *acknowledge* that God is now present, sitting in the chair beside you, ready to listen to your petitions and give you advice and direction. Finally, *acclimate* your mind, body, and heart to receive and accept His Word and direction.[1]

God is ever ready to help us seek peace and quiet in this hectic world. So enter that quiet place, remembering that when you pray, He will listen (see Jeremiah 29:12). Once you've said "Amen," remain silent and listen, for God is also ready to speak and to guide you through this life. "I will instruct you and teach you in the way you should go" (Psalm 32:8 niv). Amid His presence you will receive His courage and strength to meet the day. What a wonderful God we have!

Waiting on the Lord

Dear Lord, as I enter into this quiet time with You, calm my mind, body, and spirit. Take my hand and lead me to Your side. I long to feel Your touch, hear Your voice, and see Your face. Whatever comes to me this day, I know You will be with me, as You are now—within me, above me, beside me. Thank You for strengthening my heart. Thank You for giving me the patience to wait on You.

Wait on the Lord; be of good courage, and He shall strengthen your heart; wait, I say, on the Lord!

Psalm 27:14 NKJV

Quiet Waters

My Shepherd, my Lord, my Savior, lead me beside the still waters. Lie with me in the green pastures. Restore my soul. Lead me down the paths of Your choosing today. With You by my side, I fear no evil. You are my Comfort and my Guide. I am happy in Your presence. Your goodness and Your mercy are with me this minute, this hour, and this day. Thank You, Lord, for leading me here and making me whole—for being the Shepherd of my life.

He makes me lie down in green pastures,
he leads me beside quiet waters.
PSALM 23:2 NIV

Morning Meditation

You defend me, You love me, You lead me. How great is that! How great are You! Too wonderful for words. This morning in Your presence, I rejoice. This morning, I direct my prayers to You, knowing that You will hear my words and interpret my groans. I am directing my voice to You, Lord, and patiently await Your instructions.

Give heed to the voice of my cry, my King and my God, for to you I will pray. My voice You shall hear in the morning, O Lord; in the morning I will direct it to You, and I will look up. . . . Make Your way straight before my face.

Psalm 5:2–3, 8 NKJV

Strength in God

Lord, I know You hear my voice when I pray to You! You are my strength and my shield. When my heart trusts in You, I am overjoyed. You give me courage to meet the challenges of the day. You give me strength to do the tasks You have set before me. You build me up, raise me to the heights, and lead me to places I would never have dreamed were possible. You are the Friend who will never leave me, the Guide who walks before me. With You in my life, I can do anything.

May honor and thanks be given to the Lord, because He has heard my prayer. The Lord is my strength and my safe cover. My heart trusts in Him, and I am helped.

Psalm 28:6–7 NLV

Living Water

Lord, thank You for being with me as I spend my quiet time in Your presence. When I am in the wilderness, You tell me not to fear. You tell me to rise in Your strength. And then You open my eyes and direct me to the living water. Lord, there is no one like You, no one who loves me as You do. I thirst for Your presence and am rewarded with Your peace. Be Thou my eternal fount of blessing.

Early the next morning. . .she went on her way and wandered in the Desert. . . .
Then God opened her eyes and she saw a well of water.

GENESIS 21:14, 19 NIV

Renewal of Strength

Lord, I come to You in this early morning time, my heart at peace, my mouth at rest. As I wait upon You, You come to me, eager to talk and to listen. As I spend time here with You, my strength is renewed. I mount up with wings like eagles. With You by my side, I can run and not be weary, walk and not be faint. Be with me here and now, today and forever.

Those who hope in the Lord will renew their strength. They will soar on wings like eagles; they will run and not grow weary, they will walk and not be faint.

Isaiah 40:31 NIV

Peace Like a River

Lord, my Pilot and my Guide, give me direction this day. You teach me what is best for me and direct me in the way I should go. When I pay attention to Your commands, You give me peace like a river. It is to Your living water that I run. Help me, Lord, to obey You in all I say and do. Give me the wisdom to abide in Your Word, all to Your glory!

"I am the Lord your God, Who teaches you to do well, Who leads you in the way you should go. If only you had listened to My Laws! Then your peace would have been like a river and your right-standing with God would have been like the waves of the sea."

Isaiah 48:17–18 NLV

Morning Sustenance

Lord, although I am tired this morning, You will give me all the strength I need to meet the challenges of the day. Your Word sustains me when I am weary. You awaken me morning by morning. I am ready, Lord, to listen to Your voice. Teach me what You would have me learn today. My only desire is to bring glory to Your name, Lord. May everything I do today be pleasing in Your sight.

The Sovereign Lord has given me a well-instructed tongue, to know the word that sustains the weary. He wakens me morning by morning, wakens my ear to listen like one being instructed.

Isaiah 50:4 NIV

Rejoice!

This is the day that You have made, Lord! I will rejoice and be glad in it! Lord, I feel Your light shining upon me. I feel Your presence all around me. I glory in Your touch! No matter what comes against me today, I know that You will be with me, so there is no reason to be afraid. All I have to do is reach for You and You are here with me. You are so good to me. Thank You, Lord, for Your goodness and Your love.

This is the day which the Lord hath made; we will rejoice and be glad in it.

Psalm 118:24 KJV

God of Peace

God, sometimes life is so messy. Nothing has been going right. All I want to do is throw up my hands in frustration. But that is not of You, Lord. You are not a God of disorder but a God of peace. Help me, Lord, to be at peace now as I come to You in prayer. Help me to rest in Your presence and gain Your strength to meet the challenges of this day.

For God is not a God of disorder but of peace.

1 Corinthians 14:33 NIV

Strength for the Day

Oh God, I long for Your presence and Your touch. Deliver me from worry, fear, and distress. Bind me with Your love and forgiveness as I rest in You. Fill me with Your power and Your strength to meet the challenges of this day. Thank You, Lord, for the way You are working in my life. Keep me close to You throughout this day.

O Lord, be gracious to us; we have waited for You.
Be their strength every morning, Our salvation also in the time of distress.
Isaiah 33:2 NASB

The Power of Belief

"Everything is possible for one who believes."
Mark 9:23 NIV

Remember when the disciples saw Jesus walking on the water toward them? They thought He was a ghost and cried out in fear. But Jesus immediately said to them: "Take courage! It is I. Don't be afraid." "Lord, if it's you," Peter replied, "tell me to come to you on the water." "Come," he said. Then Peter got out of the boat, walked on the water and came toward Jesus.

Before this event occurred, Peter had already seen Jesus heal a leper, mute demoniacs, his own mother-in-law, and more. He'd even been present when Jesus demonstrated His power over nature by calming the wind. Still, after witnessing all these miracles, Peter wavered on the water.

Like Peter, when we begin to panic and find ourselves sinking, we must cry out in specific and fervent prayer to Jesus, saying, "Lord, save me!" And as Jesus did with Peter, He will *immediately* reach out and save us. By keeping our eyes off our difficulties and fixed on Jesus, we will overcome our doubts and fears and find ourselves walking on the living water of His power, His Word, and His promises. We must be unwavering in our faith that God will uphold us no matter what our trial.

Each morning, arm yourself before you step out of your boat. To keep your heart from wavering, plant these words in your heart: " 'Everything is possible for one who believes' " (Mark 9:23 NIV). Then as you pray in faith and in accordance with His will, do not doubt in your heart but believe you will have what you ask. Because Jesus promises that indeed you *will* have it! He *will* answer your prayers. He will not let you sink in the sea of doubt, fear, and despair! Just keep your eyes on Jesus and your heart in the Word, and God, in His strength, will keep you walking on the waters of great expectations.

Feeding on Faithfulness

As I dwell on this earth and take in my early morning manna, I feel Your presence beside me. I remember the times You've taken care of me, suffered with me, and led me through the darkness, and I feed on these memories. I feed on Your faithfulness.Thank You for always being there for me. Remain with me now and for the rest of this day, giving me courage and strength as I trust in You.

Trust in the Lord, and do good; dwell in the land, and feed on His faithfulness.

Psalm 37:3 NKJV

Access to Peace and Grace

It is my faith in You, Jesus, that keeps me sane and gives me peace. I am eternally grateful for that peace, and I thank You. My faith in You justifies me and gives me the grace I need to forgive others. Help me to do that today. Help me to look at those who have wounded me as You look at me—without blame and with love. Keep me in Your hand and give me Your strength as I go through this day.

Therefore, having been justified by faith, we have peace with God through our Lord Jesus Christ, through whom also we have access by faith into this grace in which we stand, and rejoice in hope of the glory of God.

ROMANS 5:1–2 NKJV

Unwavering Faith

Lord, let me be like Abraham, with unwavering faith and belief in Your promises. May I be strengthened by Your Word as I meditate on it before You today, knowing and believing that You have the power to do what You have promised. I believe that You will be with me forever, that You will never leave me nor forsake me, that You will keep my head above the water, and that You love me now and to the end of my days. Thank You, Lord, for saving my soul and strengthening my faith.

Yet [Abraham] *did not waver through unbelief regarding the promise of God, but was strengthened in his faith and gave glory to God, being fully persuaded that God had power to do what he had promised.*

Romans 4:20–21 NIV

Standing Firm

God, I don't feel very strong today. In fact, I am filled with that sinking-like-Peter feeling. Buoy my faith, Lord, so that I can stand firm. As I meditate on how You stopped the wind and calmed the sea, how just a touch of Your hand healed others, how there was power even in the hem of Your garment, I know I can stand today, firm in You. Continue filling me with Your power, courage, and strength.

Watch, stand fast in the faith, be brave, be strong.

1 Corinthians 16:13 NKJV

Living Water

Oh God, I see the waves crashing around me, my troubles overwhelming me. I feel as if I am sinking with no foothold to save me! Come to me, Lord. Cover me with Your love. Lord, I believe! Help my unbelief! I refuse to look at all the troubles around me. I will keep my eyes on You only. I see Your light and love, Your precious face, Your lips telling me, "It is I; do not be afraid. Just believe." I believe, Lord! I believe!

Our life is lived by faith. We do not live by what we see in front of us.

2 Corinthians 5:7 NLV

Strengthened in the Faith

Jesus, my Jesus, thank You for always being with me, holding me up above the waters of this life, especially when the current is more than I can bear. As You uphold me, day by day, morning by morning, my faith grows. There is no one like You, Jesus. No one like You. I am strengthened during this time with You. I overflow with thankfulness and praise. What would I ever do without You in my life?

Just as you received Christ Jesus as Lord, continue to live your lives in him, rooted and built up in him, strengthened in the faith as you were taught, and overflowing with thankfulness.

COLOSSIANS 2:6–7 NIV

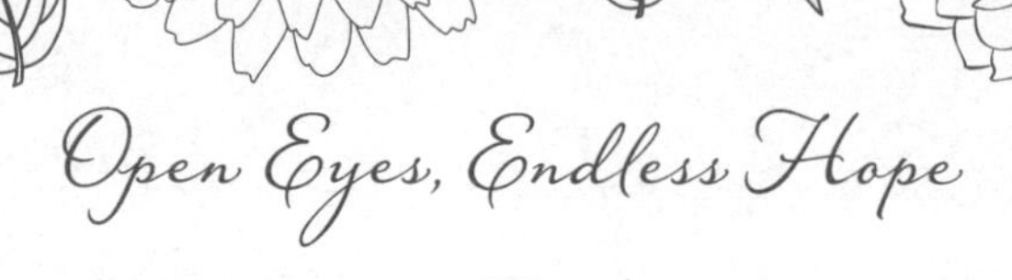

Open Eyes, Endless Hope

Each morning You open the eyes of my heart and fill me with Your awesome resurrection power. As I seek Your face, I am filled with endless hope. I revel in Your glorious riches. I am saved by the power of belief. Enlighten my mind, heart, and spirit as we spend these moments together. I await Your words, dear Lord. Speak to me now!

I pray that the eyes of your heart may be enlightened, so that you will know what is the hope of His calling, what are the riches of the glory of His inheritance in the saints, and what is the surpassing greatness of His power toward us who believe.

EPHESIANS 1:18–19 NASB

The Joy of Belief

What incredible joy fills my soul! I love You, Lord, and am filled with Your love for me. Words cannot express the glorious joy I feel at this moment, basking in Your morning light, warmed by Your presence at my side. I want You to be with me throughout this entire day. Never leave me. Never forsake me. Give me that faith that believes in things unseen!

Though you have not seen Him, you love Him, and though you do not see Him now, but believe in Him, you greatly rejoice with joy inexpressible and full of glory.

1 Peter 1:8 NASB

Firmly Anchored

Lord, I read in Your Word about the miracles that You have performed. I have seen such miracles in my own life. Help me not to give in to that sinking-like-Peter feeling, one full of doubt. Help me not to be blown and tossed by the wind but firmly anchored in the harbor of Your Word, Your love, and Your promises.

If any of you lack wisdom, let him ask of God. . . . But let him ask in faith, nothing wavering. For he that wavereth is like a wave of the sea driven with the wind and tossed.

James 1:5–6 KJV

No Doubt about It

Holy Spirit, it all comes down to faith in God. Fill my heart with assurance, with confidence, and with the promise from Jesus that everything is possible for him who believes. Clear my mind, soul, and spirit of any lingering doubts, even those that I have hidden. Allow me to rest in the confidence and belief in my Savior.

"Have faith in God. . . . For assuredly, I say to you, whoever. . . does not doubt in his heart, but believes that those things he says will be done, he will have whatever he says."

MARK 11:22–23 NKJV

Rewards of Belief

From the beginning of time, Lord, You have been the One. You are the Ancient of Days. I humbly come before You, earnestly seeking Your face. I am awed by Your presence and staggered by Your might and power. Hear my prayer, O Lord. Reward me with Your peace and Your strength. I believe in You.

But without faith it is impossible to please him: for he that cometh to God must believe that he is, and that he is a rewarder of them that diligently seek him.

Hebrews 11:6 KJV

The Power of Creative Vision

Be careful how you live. Don't live like fools, but those who are wise.
Make the most of every opportunity.
EPHESIANS 5:15–16 NLT

Many people look back upon their lives as a series of missed opportunities. Are you one of them? We cannot change the past, nor can we waste the present by lamenting over how many times we've allowed the winds of opportunity to pass us by. Don't let yourself become mired in the "would've-could've-should've" mode. Take the following steps to ensure that you make the most of every opportunity in the future.

First, *pray for creative vision*. Jesus is just waiting for you to prayerfully present your thoughts, dreams, and ideas to Him.

Second, *listen expectantly.* After you have prayed for creative vision, be still, open your mind, and *expect* God to speak to you. God shares your dreams *with* you. He is eager to project His vision for you on the plasma screen of your expectant mind.

Third, *be resourceful*. Sometimes, when God is calling us into a certain area, we need to *make* our own opportunities.

And last, *have courage*. Sometimes it seems easier to stay anchored in the place where we feel the most comfortable. But that place may not be where God wants us to be (see Deuteronomy 1:6–7 NIV). Courage is needed to set sail into unknown waters.

Don't let your ship of life rot in dry dock. Pray for creative vision, expect God to speak to you, be resourceful, and then courageously set sail. Through it all, remember that you are never alone: God and His creative wisdom will be with you throughout your voyage, steering you through every ocean of life!

Walking in God's Wisdom

Lord, I want to do what You have created me to do. I come to You today, seeking Your direction for my life. I have my own ideas of how You want me to serve You, to enlarge Your kingdom here on earth, to provide for myself, my family, and my church. But I need Your wisdom. Which route should I take? When shall I begin? How shall I go? Lead me, Lord, into the waters You have chartered for my life.

Listen, my son, and accept what I say, and the years of your life will be many. I instruct you in the way of wisdom and lead you along straight paths. When you walk, your steps will not be hampered; when you run, you will not stumble. Hold on to instruction, do not let it go; guard it well, for it is your life.

PROVERBS 4:10–13 NIV

Wisdom of Creation

God, Your creation is so awesome. Everywhere I look, I see Your handiwork. You have made it all. You have made me. Continue to mold me and shape me into the person You want me to be. Give me knowledge and wisdom in how best to serve You.

By wisdom the Lord laid the earth's foundations, by understanding he set the heavens in place; by his knowledge the watery depths were divided, and the clouds let drop the dew.

Proverbs 3:19–20 NIV

Master of Creation

Jesus, Jesus, Jesus. I am still this morning, before You, waiting to seek Your face, Your direction, Your wisdom, Your ideas for my life. You are the master of creation. You are in me, with me, above me, below me. You have made me. Now make of my life what You will.

In the beginning was the Word. . . . All things were made by him; and without him was not any thing made that was made.

John 1:1, 3 KJV

Asked to Be Co-creators

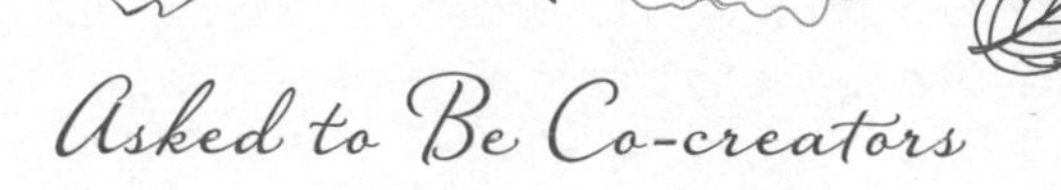

Lord, You formed all things. And afterward, You invited man to be Your co-creator, allowing him to name things, do things, and serve You. Show me now, Lord, how You want me to employ my talents, my gifts, and myself to make this world a better place. Come to me now, Lord. Imprint upon my mind what You want me to do, which door You want me to walk through.

And out of the ground the LORD God formed every beast of the field, and every fowl of the air; and brought them unto Adam to see what he would call them: and whatsoever Adam called every living creature, that was the name thereof.

GENESIS 2:19 KJV

Faith in the Invisible

I cannot see my future, Lord. I must trust in Your wisdom to guide me through these unchartered waters. Although I cannot see what the future holds, You see it, Lord. You have it all planned out. Open my ears to Your voice and my eyes to Your creative vision for my life. Help me to see where You want me to go. Then give me the courage to steer my life in that direction.

By faith we understand that the worlds were prepared by the word of God, so that what is seen was not made out of things which are visible.

HEBREWS 11:3 NASB

The Breath of Life

It is through You that I have life. Each and every day, You breathe life into my soul. You send my spirit soaring into unknown heights. Thank You for the gift of life. I dedicate it to Your service. Where would You like me to go? What shall I do? Which path shall I take? Speak to me as I remain still, listening for Your voice, awaiting Your direction.

The LORD God formed man of the dust of the ground, and breathed into his nostrils the breath of life; and man became a living soul.

GENESIS 2:7 KJV

The Right Focus

Help me, Lord, to focus on You in all I say and do, in every decision I make, and in every direction I take. Help me to make the most of each opportunity. My life's aim is to serve, obey, and seek You. I do not know what to do, but my eyes, Lord, are upon Your heavenly face, and in this I rejoice!

We do not know what to do, but our eyes are upon You.
2 Chronicles 20:12 AMP

Advancing for God

You have given me direction. It is time for me to move forward, to sail into unknown waters. You have commanded me to advance. You have already given me the land beyond these seas. All I need to do is sail toward You and take possession of the blessings You have provided. Thank You, God, for allowing me to be a part of Your master plan.

The Lord our God said to us at Horeb, "You have stayed long enough at this mountain. Break camp and advance. . . . See, I have given you this land. Go in and take possession. . . ."
Deuteronomy 1:6–8 niv

You Made Me!

You have known me since the beginning. You know my doubts and fears, yet You love me still. Sometimes I feel as if I am adrift in confusion. I need You to lovingly urge me on past that darkness and into Your light. Thank You for Your patience. Help me to create a life with You; help me to be not just a lump of clay sitting on a shelf, out of harm's way but unused. Continue to shape me and mold me into the person You want me to be.

Thy hands have made me and fashioned me.

Psalm 119:73 KJV

Set Apart and Appointed

Oh God, before I was even conceived, You knew me and loved me. You have set me apart for a special purpose, for a way to achieve Your ends. I am nothing without You, yet You ask me to be a part of the grand plan. Even knowing my weaknesses, You have loved me. Give me the vision You have for my life so that I may best know how to serve You. Here I am, Lord. Use me!

"Before I formed you in the womb I knew you,
before you were born I set you apart; I appointed you."
JEREMIAH 1:5 NIV

No Fear

You've made me the way I am for a reason, for a purpose. You are the Author and the Finisher of my faith. For now and always You are there to help me. I am not afraid when my hand is in Yours. Thank You for leading me out of the darkness and into the light of Your Word.

This is what the LORD says—he who made you, who formed you in the womb, and who will help you: Do not be afraid.

ISAIAH 44:2 NIV

The Power of Divine Guidance

For the Lord will go before you.
Isaiah 52:12 NIV

When I was a child struggling with my future, my grandmother gave me the "gift" of a worry stone. Holding this flat, oval-shaped, polished gemstone between her fingers and thumb, Grandma showed me how to rub the stone. She said that when I did this, I would gain relief from the concerns that plagued me.

As the years went by, I began to realize that it didn't matter how much I used the worry stone, because it changed neither the present nor the future. So I put the stone away. . .but kept the worries close at hand.

Then, years later, I began diving into God's Word with an unquenchable thirst. As I read I discovered the powerful words of Jeremiah 29:11–12: " 'For I know the plans I have for you,' declares the Lord, 'plans to prosper you and not to harm you, plans to give you hope and a future. Then you will call upon me and come and pray to me, and I will listen to you' " (NIV).

I was awestruck. God had plans for me! Plans to prosper and not to harm me! Plans to give me hope and a future! I realized that when worries began to come upon me, all I had to do was call upon Him, seek Him with all my heart, and tell Him all my fears of the future. He would listen and then lead me to go in the power of His divine guidance, urging me to be confident that He is before me, guiding me.

Oh, if only Grandma had given me the gift of scripture instead of a worry stone! How many years I wasted in the pit of despair over what-ifs, girded only with the tool of a worry stone instead of God's Word.

When worries about the future plague you, delve into God's Word, turn your heart to seek His face, and pray to the Lord your Savior who never ceases to "instruct you and teach you in the way you should go" and "guide you with [His] eye" (Psalm 32:8 NKJV). Ask God to give you the power of His divine guidance, helping you fulfill His plan for your life.

My Desires

Lord, as I come before You today, delighting in Your presence, I ask for Your divine guidance. You know the desires of my heart—to know, love, and live in You. Show me the way You want me to go. Give me the courage to face the future, knowing that because You go before me, I need never be afraid.

Delight thyself also in the Lord; and he shall give thee the desires of thine heart.

Psalm 37:4 KJV

Serving with Purpose

Dearest God, You have a purpose for my life. You have plans to prosper me. I put my life, my heart, my spirit, and my soul in Your safe hands, this minute, this hour, this day. Within Your firm grasp, I need not worry about what tomorrow may bring. I know You have my life planned. I just need to keep close to You and to keep walking in Your way, looking neither to the right nor the left but straight ahead toward You.

"David. . .served the purpose of God in his own generation."
ACTS 13:36 NASB

Loved Now and Forever

No matter what happens, Lord, I cannot be separated from You and Your love. Oh, what that means to me! Fill me with the love that never ends. May it flow through me and reach those I meet this day. May my future be filled with blessing upon blessing, and may I praise You today and in the days to come.

I am convinced that neither death nor life, neither angels nor demons, neither the present nor the future, nor any powers, neither height nor depth, nor anything else in all creation, will be able to separate us from the love of God that is in Christ Jesus our Lord.

Romans 8:38–39 NIV

A Future for Me

Lord, I am Your child, a child of peace. When someone strikes me on the left cheek, I turn my head and give them the other. I can only do this through Your power. Nothing can harm me when I am living so close to You. Now, with the next breath I take, give me the gift of stillness, of silence, as I put my future, my hopes, my dreams into Your capable hands.

Consider the blameless, observe the upright;
a future awaits those who seek peace.
Psalm 37:37 NIV

Sweet Wisdom Breeds Hope

You, O Lord, give me hope for the future. Your presence fills me. I seek Your wisdom to renew my spirit and help me face the challenges of this life. I have great expectations. I believe that You are working in my life and good things await me today. May I further the plans for Your kingdom as You lead me through this life and time.

So shall the knowledge of wisdom be unto thy soul: when thou hast found it, then there shall be a reward, and thy expectation shall not be cut off.

Proverbs 24:14 KJV

In God's Arms!

No matter what I face today, You, Lord, are going before me. You appear before my very eyes. You will lead me through the desert, sustaining me with Your living water. When I am tired, You will carry me like a child, until I reach the place You have intended for me.

Then I said to you, "Do not be terrified; do not be afraid of them. The Lord your God, who is going before you, will fight for you, as he did for you in Egypt, before your very eyes, and in the desert. There you saw how the Lord your God carried you, as a father carries his son, all the way you went until you reached this place."

Deuteronomy 1:29–31 NIV

A Future Hope

Nothing will cause me dismay, nothing will discourage me with You by my side, O Lord of my life. Help me to seek Your advice, Your Word, before I speak, before I move, before I act. Guide me through this maze of life, Lord, with the assurance that You always walk before me. Embed this truth deep within my soul.

There is surely a future hope for you, and your hope will not be cut off.

PROVERBS 23:18 NIV

No Fear for the Future

Do not allow my foot to stumble, Lord. Eliminate the obstacles of worry and fear that line the path before me. Give me hope and courage to face my future. Give me a clear mind to make the right decisions. And, at the end of this day, give me the peace of sweet slumber as I lie down within Your mighty arms.

Keep sound wisdom and discretion: So shall they be life unto thy soul, and grace to thy neck. Then shalt thou walk in thy way safely, and thy foot shall not stumble. When thou liest down, thou shalt not be afraid: yea, thou shalt lie down, and thy sleep shall be sweet.

PROVERBS 3:21–24 KJV

Unknown Future

Dear God, I don't know what lies before me. I feel plagued by the what-ifs that tumble through my mind and pierce my confident spirit. Allow me to let You fill my soul. Help me to be confident in Your wisdom and power to guide me, so that, although You have concealed from me the knowledge of future events, I may be ready for any changes that may come.

Indeed, how can people avoid what they don't know is going to happen?

Ecclesiastes 8:7 NLT

Strengthened Hearts

Your eyes, Lord, are ranging throughout the earth. You see it all, Lord, the past, the present, the future. You are the God that was, is, and will be. You are constantly looking out for me because my heart is fully committed to You. Help me to rest in the assurance that Your arms will always uphold me. I want to be with You forever and ever.

"For the eyes of the LORD move to and fro throughout the earth that He may strongly support those whose heart is completely His."
2 CHRONICLES 16:9 NASB

God's Plans

You have led me to this place where I now lie before You, seeking Your presence and Your face, Your guidance and Your strength. Your plans for my life stand firm, although they are as yet unrevealed to me. With one glance, You see all the generations that have gone before, that are present now, and that will come in the future. You see it all! Allow me to rest in the knowledge that each and every day You go before me, and that in the end, all will be well with my soul.

But the plans of the Lord stand firm forever,
the purposes of his heart through all generations.
PSALM 33:11 NIV

The Power of Persistent, Specific, Expectant Petition

So I say to you, Ask and keep on asking and it shall be given you; seek and keep on seeking and you shall find; knock and keep on knocking and the door shall be opened to you.

LUKE 11:9 AMP

When we had to have our dog Schaefer put down, my family and I were heartbroken. That night and the next morning, I asked God to heal us from our grief and give us a new, healthy puppy to love. I continued this petition every morning in my quiet time with God.

Now I told God that I didn't care what the puppy looked like, only that it be a healthy, loving, face-licking, eager-and-able-to-go-for-a-walk pound puppy. I also asked God for patience, to give me a waiting yet joyfully confident, expectant heart.

Just when we had about given up hope, my husband, Pete, urged my son Zach and me to check out the last puppy left at a local dog rescue facility. As we walked up the long driveway of Dogs for Adoption, a wrinkly-headed, yellow-haired puppy came loping along on the heels of one of the rescue workers. As he ran to my son, he first licked his face and then nibbled on his ear, turning my sixteen-year-old teenager into a giggling, joyous boy. It was love at first sight.

That afternoon we brought home a healthy, loving, face-licking, eager-and-able-to-go-for-a-walk, yet amazingly funny-looking, mischievous puppy. In His timing and in His way, God answered my persistent, specific, expectant petitions.

Harness the power of persistent, specific, expectant petitions. Present your needs to God today and every day—ask and keep on asking—remembering the words of Andrew Murray: "Let prayer be not only the utterance of your desires, but a fellowship with God, until we know by faith that our prayers are heard."[2]

Financial Aid

Here I am, Lord, coming to You to ask You to fill my needs, to help me to support my family financially. God, You know these are hard times, You know how much money this household needs to function each day, week, and month. Hear my prayer and help me to do my part in providing for my family. I thank You for this roof over our heads. And now I humbly beseech You to help us meet our needs.

You do not have, because you do not ask God.

JAMES 4:2 NIV

Christ's Riches

Oh, Lord, what a promise You have made to me, that You will supply all I need through Christ. He is my Good Shepherd; with Him I shall not want! Help me to rest confidently in the assurance that in Your time my prayers will be answered. Let my prayer time be more than utterances of what I desire but a time of fellowship with You, knowing that You will provide what I need.

My God shall supply all your need according to His riches in glory by Christ Jesus.

PHILIPPIANS 4:19 NKJV

Watching with Hope

I watch and wait expectantly, Lord, for You to answer the petitions I make to You today. I bring them to You mindful of the way You are always there, ready to listen, ready to advise, ready to answer. Give me the gift of patience as I wait for Your response. Help me not to run ahead of You but to wait and pray and hope.

But as for me, I watch in hope for the Lord,
I wait for God my Savior; my God will hear me.
Micah 7:7 NIV

Morning Requests

Lord, here I am this morning, coming before You once again. I know You hear my voice, but You even understand my groans and know my unspoken thoughts. In this stillness, I present my requests to You and I look to You for a reply. I watch for Your presence to come near me. I wait for You to speak to my heart, knowing that You only want what's best for me. Thank You for being my loving, patient, and just heavenly Father.

In the morning You hear my voice, O Lord; in the morning I prepare [a prayer, a sacrifice] for You and watch and wait [for You to speak to my heart].

Psalm 5:3 AMP

In His Time

Lord, sometimes I don't understand why it takes so long for You to answer some of my prayers. At times Your answers are immediate, but on other occasions, I need to keep coming before You, asking over and over again for You to meet my need. Help me to grow during this time, Lord. Give me the confidence to ask and keep on asking.

The Lord upholdeth all that fall, and raiseth up all those that be bowed down. The eyes of all wait upon thee; and thou givest them their meat in due season. Thou openest thine hand, and satisfiest the desire of every living thing.

Psalm 145:14–16 KJV

Day by Day

You know what I need, Lord, and I am here before You again this morning, asking You to meet those needs. As food prices continue to rise, I need Your help more and more to feed my family. Help me to fill those mouths with that which You have so graciously blessed me.

Give us day by day our daily bread.

Luke 11:3 KJV

God's Goodness

Lord, I come to You this morning, thanking You for giving me all that I need each and every day. I have endured some lean times in the past, but right now, things are looking up, and it's all because I looked up—to You! Help me to keep my focus upon You and not on what I lack.

"God has been very gracious to me. I have more than enough."
GENESIS 33:11 NLT

Lifting Manna

Here I am once more, Lord, asking You again this morning to meet my needs. I've been so down, Lord, with all the things that have been happening in the world, in my home, in my family. Help me again today to go forth, to gather as much as I need and be content with that. Hear my prayer, O Lord, and help me day by day.

Each morning everyone gathered as much as they needed.

Exodus 16:21 NIV

Boundless Grace

Lord, because of You, I have all I need. You continually shower blessings upon me to the point where they are overflowing. With Your support, I can finally stand on my own two feet. I even have enough left over to give to others and to do the work that You have called me to do. Thank You, Father, for blessing my life.

God is able to make all grace (every favor and earthly blessing) come to you in abundance, so that you may always and under all circumstances and whatever the need be self-sufficient [possessing enough to require no aid or support and furnished in abundance for every good work and charitable donation].

2 Corinthians 9:8 AMP

Wounded Hearts

I hate being so needy, Lord, so poor, so hurt, so wounded. Troubles plague me on each and every side every time I try to depend upon myself to meet all my needs. Today I come to You, the source of all power. Grant me my petitions. Help me to rest assured that You are taking care of me, and that as long as I abide in You, all will be well.

For I am poor and needy, and my heart is wounded within me.

Psalm 109:22 KJV

Bold Petitioners

I boldly come to You this morning, knowing that You will give me as much as I need because of Your love for me. Thank You for guiding me, giving me wisdom, and teaching me patience. You have blessed me before, and I am confident that You will continue to bless me as I serve You.

"I tell you, even though he will not get up and give him anything because he is his friend, yet because of his persistence he will get up and give him as much as he needs."

LUKE 11:8 NASB

The Power of Adoration

Give thanks to him and praise his name.
Psalm 100:4 NLT

What a privilege to approach God, to bow down before Him, laud Him with our praises, and feel His presence within us! Sometimes, as we draw near, appropriate words evade us. Yet all is not lost, for God has given us a powerful, praise-filled resource—the book of Psalms.

In the midst of praising our Lord and Savior, our lives are transformed in several ways. First and foremost, our spirits become intimately connected with His. As we lift our voices, extolling His name and deeds, we are invaded by His presence. "But You are holy, O You Who dwell in [the holy place where]. . .praises. . .[are offered]" (Psalm 22:3 AMP). God abides within us when we praise Him!

Second, when we praise God our fears are allayed. Psalm 56:10–11 says, "In God, whose word I praise, in the Lord, whose word I praise—in God I trust and am not afraid" (NIV). There is no room for fear where praise has taken up residence.

Third, praise changes our outlook as we view our world through the eyes of our Creator. "Praise the Lord from the heavens. . . . Let [His angels, heavenly hosts, sun, moon, stars, highest heavens, waters above the skies] praise the name of the Lord, for he commanded and they were created" (Psalm 148:1, 5 NIV). Suddenly, when we see things from the perspective of the One who made and sustains the entire universe, the cares of this world grow dim.

And finally, our love for God is deepened when we adore Him and give Him thanks for past blessings.

After the sun rises but before you approach God with your daily petitions, get into the praise mode, reminding Him (and yourself) how terrific He really is, how awed you are to have Him in your life, how blessed you are that He came down to earth to save *you*. As you speak to your Creator, through His Word, He will speak to you.

Shouting for Joy!

Your hands created the heavens and the earth. You breathed upon Adam and gave him life. Everything that was created was created through Your Son, Jesus Christ. The trees, the earth, the waters, and the creatures clap their hands in praise to You. This is the day that You have made! I will rejoice and be glad in it as I shout Your name to the heavens!

Be glad in the Lord and rejoice, you righteous;
and shout for joy, all you upright in heart!
Psalm 32:11 NKJV

Praising in Song

My heart rejoices in Your presence this morning! To Your ears, Lord, I pray that my singing will be a joyful noise. Your grace is amazing. You are my all in all, I worship and adore You. Lean down Your ear to me as I sing about Your love, for how great Thou art, Lord! How great Thou art!

My heart greatly rejoiceth; and with my song will I praise him.

Psalm 28:7 KJV

An Answer to My Cry

Dear God, You have done so many things for me, saved me from so many dangers, toils, and snares. I cry out to You again this morning. Fill me with Your Spirit. Touch me with Your presence. And as I go through this day, may I be so filled with Your praises that I cannot help but tell others what You have done for me!

Come and hear, all you who fear God; let me tell you what he has done for me.
I cried out to him with my mouth; his praise was on my tongue. . . .
God has surely listened and heard my prayer. Praise be to God!
PSALM 66:16–17, 19–20 NIV

By His Great Mercy

Lord, I humble myself before You, bowing down at Your throne. You are so great, so awesome. Your presence fills this universe. I am filled with Your amazing love, touched by Your compassion. There is no one like You in my life, my Master, my Lord, my God.

In the morning, Lord, you hear my voice. . . . I, by your great love. . . can come into your house; in reverence I bow down toward your holy temple.

Psalm 5:3, 7 niv

His Awesome Power

Lord, You parted the Red Sea and You still the wind and the waves. You give sight to the blind and hearing to the deaf. You raise people from the dead. Your power is awesome. Nothing is impossible for You. I bow before You, singing praises to Your name.

Say to God, "How awesome are your deeds! So great is your power. . . . All the earth bows down to you; they sing praise to you, they sing praise to your name."

Psalm 66:3–4 niv

Praise for Deliverance

You are the Good Shepherd, the All-Sufficient One, my Rock of Refuge. You hold the universe in Your hands and yet You are concerned with everything going on in my life. I am staggered by Your love and faithfulness to me. You continually draw me up into Your presence. You deliver me from the depths of darkness.

I will praise you, Lord my God, with all my heart; I will glorify your name forever. For great is your love toward me; you have delivered me from the depths.

Psalm 86:12–13 NIV

No Fear When God Is Near

Your instruction keeps me on the right path and for that I praise You. Thank You for giving me Your Holy Word, to have and to hold. With Your Word I can speak to You and You can speak to me. You are the Great Communicator of my life. I trust in Your Word, for when I am armed with it, I have no fear.

In God will I praise his word: in the Lord will I praise his word.
In God have I put my trust: I will not be afraid what man can do unto me.
Psalm 56:10–11 KJV

Heart-Filled Praise

As I sit here before You, my heart reaches out to touch You, the great God, seated in the heavenlies. Meld my spirit with Yours so that our wills are one. Your love and faithfulness are tremendous. I praise You, Lord, with my lips, my voice, my mouth, my life.

I will praise thee with my whole heart. . . . I will worship toward thy holy temple, and praise thy name for thy lovingkindness and for thy truth: for thou hast magnified thy word above all thy name.

Psalm 138:1–2 KJV

Lifelong Praise

At this moment and throughout this day, I sing my praises to You, O God. Music is one of Your gifts and I thank You for it. As my spirit in song rises to join with Yours, may I continually be reminded of all You are, of all You have done, and all You will do.

I will sing unto the LORD as long as I live:
I will sing praise to my God while I have my being.
PSALM 104:33 KJV

Praise to the Heavenly Creator

You made all the planets, all the stars, the waters on the earth, the land on which I stand. Is there nothing too difficult for You? You are wrapped in light, and I come now into that light, to be with You, to revel in Your presence, to praise Your holy name. Surround me with Your arms among these clouds.

Bless the Lord, O my soul! O Lord my God, You are very great: You are clothed with honor and majesty, who cover Yourself with light as with a garment, who stretch out the heavens like a curtain. He lays the beams of His upper chambers in the waters, who makes the clouds His chariot, who walks on the wings of the wind.

Psalm 104:1–3 NKJV

Praise for His Gifts!

I am in high spirits today, Lord. You have provided all that I need and more! Along with my earthly needs, You have provided me with grace, spiritual gifts, love, forgiveness, Your Word, Your Son. My heart is so light. I come to You singing praises and I leave with a smile on my lips. In Your presence, my spirit is lifted. Praise the Lord!

Sing to God, sing praises to His name, cast up a highway for Him Who rides through the deserts—His name is the Lord—be in high spirits and glory before Him!

Psalm 68:4 AMP

The Power of Compassion

Therefore, as God's chosen people, holy and dearly loved, clothe yourselves with compassion, kindness, humility, gentleness and patience.
Colossians 3:12 NIV

Compassion is defined by *Merriam-Webster's Dictionary* as "sympathetic consciousness of others' distress together with a desire to alleviate it." Our God is the Father of compassion. He had so much sympathy for our suffering that He sent His one and only Son to die for us (see John 3:16). Do you share God's compassion?

Some of us, when our tender hearts see the troubles of others, may think we are too far away or too powerless to help. But that is an untruth. Our prayers are full of heavenly power. We can be on our knees in our living rooms and reach a president in the White House, a homeless man on a city street, children starving in North Korea, missionaries in South America, or an AIDS worker in Africa. With the power of compassion combined with prayer, *we can make a difference*!

When you hear of distress in the world and your heart responds with compassion, get down on your knees and pray with persistence. And if so led, take direct action. Be filled with confidence that God will work in the situation.

In this world, Jesus says we will have trouble. When things seem hopeless, we must be confident that Christ will meet us in the fire, as He did Shadrach, Meshach, and Abednego. When terror seems to reign on every side, continue faithfully onward, remembering that "if we are thrown into the blazing furnace, the God we serve is able to deliver us from it, and he will deliver us" (Daniel 3:17 NIV). Because of His unfailing compassion, we will not be consumed (see Lamentations 3:22).

The Father of Compassion

Lord, You love us so much. Fill me with that love to overflowing. Give me a compassionate heart. Lead me to the concern You would like me to champion for You, whether it be working in a soup kitchen, helping the homeless, or adopting a missionary couple. Lead me in prayer as I go down on my knees and intercede for others in distress.

Blessed be the God and Father of our Lord Jesus Christ, the Father of mercies and God of all comfort.

2 Corinthians 1:3 NKJV

Perseverance in Prayer

I feel like I've been praying forever for a situation that does not seem to be changing, Lord. I feel like Job: Here I am on my knees in prayer while the entire world dissolves around me. But I know that You are in control. You know all things. So once again, I lift my concern up to You, confident that You will handle the situation in Your timing.

As you know, we count as blessed those who have persevered. You have heard of Job's perseverance and have seen what the Lord finally brought about. The Lord is full of compassion and mercy.

James 5:11 NIV

God's Hand Guarding Us

Lord, sometimes I feel like Captain Kirk. When faced with the evils of this world, I want to say, "Beam me up, God!" But I know that no matter what happens in this world, Your hand is guarding us. And armed with Your compassion, we have the power to intercede for the hungry, the oppressed, the imprisoned, the homeless, the wounded.

I pray not that thou shouldest take them out of the world, but that thou shouldest keep them from the evil. They are not of the world, even as I am not of the world. . . . As thou hast sent me into the world, even so have I also sent them into the world.

JOHN 17:15–16, 18 KJV

Reigning Peace

Dear God, how I pray for peace around the world. Some say it's impossible—but with You all things are possible. And while peace may not yet reign throughout the earth, with You in my heart, peace reigns within, for You have overcome the world! May all people feel Your peace within!

[Jesus said,] *These things I have spoken unto you, that in me ye might have peace. In the world ye shall have tribulation: but be of good cheer; I have overcome the world.*

John 16:33 KJV

Forgiveness and Healing

God, through the divine power of Your Spirit and Your Word, I pray for my neighborhood. Demolish the stronghold of evil within this community. Touch each heart with Your peace and understanding. You know what each family needs. Help me to be an encouragement to them. Be with me as I take a prayer walk around this neighborhood, lifting each family up to Your heavenly throne.

The weapons we fight with are not the weapons of the world. On the contrary, they have divine power to demolish strongholds.

2 Corinthians 10:4 NIV

Comfort for the Suffering

Dearest Christ, I pray for Your bright, shining light to spread out into the world. For Your love to reach the ends of the earth. Give comfort to those who suffer from abuse and violence. Touch them with Your healing light and guard them with Your protective hand. Give them assurance that You are there. Allow them to feel Your presence, hear Your voice, feel Your touch.

[Jesus said,] *"You are the light of the world—*
like a city on a hilltop that cannot be hidden."
MATTHEW 5:14 NLT

Victory for Youth

Lord, I pray that You would oust the unseen evils from this land, that Your angels would battle fiercely against the dark forces corrupting our youth. Empower our youth leaders to claim a victory for young hearts. Show me how I can help at my church, how I can lead teens to You. Give parents the right words to say when dealing with their children.

For our struggle is not against flesh and blood, but against the rulers, against the powers, against the world forces of this darkness, against the spiritual forces of wickedness in the heavenly places.

Ephesians 6:12 NASB

Missionaries and Pastors

I pray for others with the confidence that You, dear Lord, hear my prayer. That although at times this world seems so unsettled, Your hand is upon our missionaries and pastors, guarding them when they are awake and as they sleep. Give them the strength to do what You have called them to do. Give them the means to help the lost, starving, diseased, and imprisoned. Give them wisdom as they reveal Your Word and reach into the darkness to spread Your light.

"If it be so, our God whom we serve is able to deliver us from the furnace of blazing fire; and He will deliver us."

DANIEL 3:17 NASB

Message of Eternal Life

The world may pass away, but Your love never fails. Those who believe in You will live with You forever. What a blessed thing! I pray that others around the world will hear the message so that they, too, can accept Your gift of eternal life. Show me how I can help spread the message, all to Your glory.

The world and its desires pass away,
but whoever does the will of God lives forever.

1 John 2:17 NIV

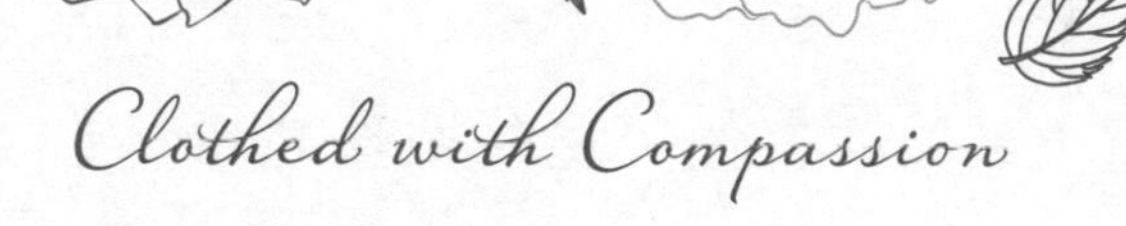

Clothed with Compassion

As I get down on my knees, I wrap myself within the cloak of compassion. I bring to You specific concerns for which You have led me to pray, knowing that You hear my prayer, confident that You will answer. And as I rise from the place of prayer, may Your kindness, humility, gentleness, and patience shine through me and lighten the hearts of others. I want to be Your servant. Help me to change the world.

Therefore, as God's chosen people, holy and dearly loved, clothe yourselves with compassion, kindness, humility, gentleness and patience.

Colossians 3:12 NIV

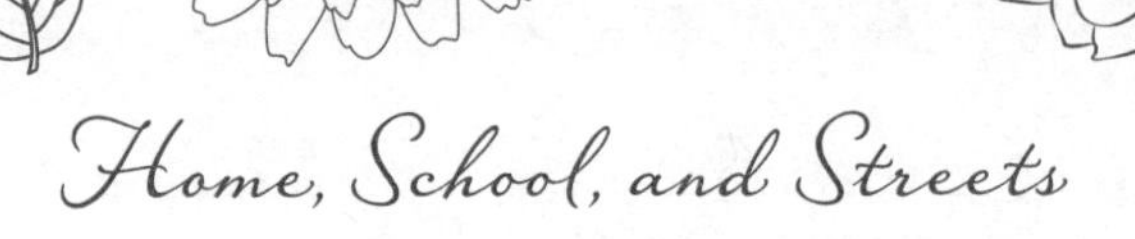

Home, School, and Streets

Lord, there are so many dark forces within our schools, on the streets, and even in our homes. I pray for Your light to eliminate the evil among us. I know that no matter what, You will prevail, dear Jesus. You have overcome this world. You have the power to do the impossible. Show me how I can make this world a better place. Give me the heart to intercede for others and the courage to step in when and where I am needed.

You are of God, little children, and have overcome them, because He who is in you is greater than he who is in the world.

1 John 4:4 NKJV

The Power of Active Faith

Faith by itself, if it is not accompanied by action, is dead.
James 2:17 niv

E. M. Bounds writes, "In carrying on his great work in the world, God works through human agents. He works through his church collectively and through his people individually. In order that they might be effective agents, they must be 'vessels unto honor, sanctified, and meet for the master's use, and prepared unto every good work.' "

Sound scary? Feeling as if you're not "holy" enough to serve others? Relax. You are *already* holy and sanctified because you have faith in Jesus Christ and have accepted Him as your Savior (see 1 Corinthians 1:2; Ephesians 1:4). Through Christ, God created you and set you apart to do good works (see Ephesians 2:10).

So it appears there is no excuse for *not* serving God. Perhaps the problem is that we are not sure what God has called us to do. Not even Paul was certain as to his role in God's plan. "What shall I do, Lord?" he asked. And God answered, "Get up. . .and go into Damascus. There you will be told all that you have been assigned to do." (See Acts 22:10.)

God has an assignment for each and every one of us. All we have to do is ask Him where and how He would like us to serve. Our gifts need not be limited to those listed in 1 Corinthians 12:8–10. The Church also needs those gifted in writing, music, hospitality, teaching, preaching, intercessory prayer, and missions, to name a few.

God doesn't want you just sitting in the pew every Sunday as you watch others ministering to your needs. According to His plan, although you are important to Him, it's not all about *you*. It's all about *God*. Find your spiritual gifts, ones that you love to use, so that you will be filled with a passion to serve. And then use them to God's great glory.

Living Sacrifices

Here I am, Lord, lifting myself up to You this morning. I want to serve You. I live to please You, for I love You with all my strength, soul, mind, heart, and body. I dedicate myself, my time, and my service to You. Show me the path You want me to take so that at the end of my days, when I see Your smiling face, You will say, "She did what she could."

Therefore, I urge you, brothers and sisters, in view of God's mercy, to offer your bodies as a living sacrifice, holy and pleasing to God—this is your true and proper worship.

Romans 12:1 NIV

Finding Your Gift

Lord, I'm looking for direction. I'm not sure how You want me to serve You. So many times I feel so inadequate, that others can do things better than I ever could. But I know those feelings are not of You. Help me to understand, Lord, how You want me to serve, what You want me to do. Not worrying about pleasing others but pleasing You, I will do so all to Your glory.

Don't act thoughtlessly, but understand what the Lord wants you to do.

Ephesians 5:17 NLT

Serving from the Heart

I want to work for You, Lord, using all my heart, soul, and talent. I want to be Your tool, serving You with passion. And as I do so, help me to keep my eye and focus on You, and not on the gift You have given me. Help me to understand what You have shaped me to do.

As slaves of Christ, do the will of God with all your heart.

Ephesians 6:6 NLT

Created for Good Works

You have shaped me into the unique person I am today. You have created me to do good works. I am awed that You prepared things in advance for me to do. From the very beginning, You made me for a specific job in Your kingdom. Give me the courage to take hold of that task. Help me not to shy away from the challenges that face me.

We are God's masterpiece. He has created us anew in Christ Jesus, so we can do the good things he planned for us long ago.

EPHESIANS 2:10 NLT

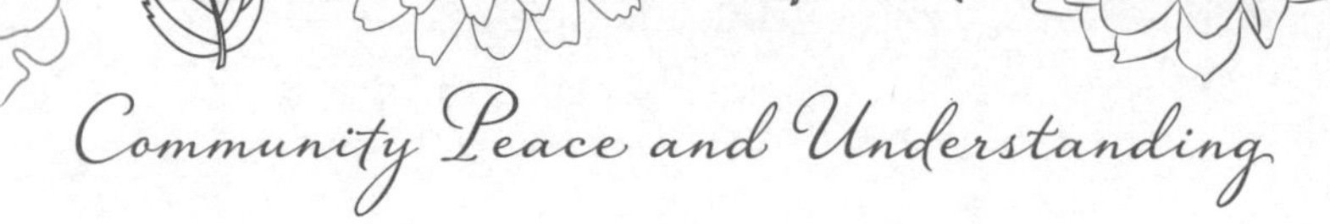

Community Peace and Understanding

Give me the humility You had when You washed the feet of the disciples. I am willing to take on whatever task—high or low—that You have for me. Grant me the spirit of cooperation as I work with others. Show me to how to use my gift in new and different ways. I serve to bring glory and honor and blessing to You.

There are different kinds of gifts, but the same Spirit distributes them. There are different kinds of service, but the same Lord. There are different kinds of working, but in all of them and in everyone it is the same God at work.

1 Corinthians 12:4–6 NIV

On Assignment from God

I come to You this morning asking for today's assignment. How would You have me serve You? Should I join the worship team? Should I become a prayer partner? Should I help in children's church? Show me the way that lies before me, Lord, so I can best serve You and others.

The Lord has assigned to each his task.

1 Corinthians 3:5 NIV

Serving the Lord

Some days, Lord, I feel as if I am working to please others and not You. But that's not what it is all about. It is You I am serving, only You. You give me the power to do Your will. It is from You that I receive my reward for a job well done. Thank You, God, for giving me the opportunity to serve You and You alone!

Whatever you do, do your work heartily, as for the Lord rather than for men, knowing that from the Lord you will receive the reward of the inheritance. It is the Lord Christ whom you serve.

Colossians 3:23–24 NASB

Servants on Fire

Give me the passion, Lord, to serve You with the gifts You have given me. Reignite the enthusiasm I felt when I first began to serve You. Help me to forget about myself and to see only You. Help me to feel Your presence within me. Set me on fire for You and You alone!

Fan into flame the gift of God, which is in you.

2 TIMOTHY 1:6 NIV

Working as One

Together we serve You, each one of us bringing our own unique gifts to lay at Your feet. Help me to do my best for You, to bring You glory, to spread Your light and Your love all around me and upon everything I touch.

In Christ we, though many, form one body, and each member belongs to all the others. We have different gifts, according to the grace given to each of us.

ROMANS 12:5–6 NIV

Honoring God

Remind me, Lord, that my service to You is a way to honor You with my body. You have done so much for me that it is overwhelming at times. Allow me to use my gift to bring greater glory to Your name so that others will be drawn ever closer to You.

God bought you with a high price. So you must honor God with your body.

1 Corinthians 6:20 NLT

Joyful Service

What an awesome privilege to serve others! I welcome this opportunity. I go into my ministry with a smile on my face and a psalm in my heart. Thank You, God, for allowing me to do for others what You have done for me. I am so blessed!

Serve the Lord with gladness.
Psalm 100:2 NKJV

The Power of Christ and His Sufficient Grace

[Christ] *said to me, "My grace is sufficient for you, for My strength is made perfect in weakness." Therefore most gladly I will rather boast in my infirmities, that the power of Christ may rest upon me. . . . For when I am weak, then I am strong.*

2 CORINTHIANS 12:9–10 NKJV

When we trust God, pray in His name, allow Him to transform us, rest in His loving arms, turn to Him for strength, and cling to the truth of His Word, we can find power and blessing even in the midst of our infirmities.

In sickness and in health, fortify your faith and strengthen your spirit by spending time in prayer, reading God's Word, and memorizing scripture. When feeling well, take care of your physical body by eating right, having regular check-ups, and getting plenty of exercise.

Each day allow Christ to enter into your life, to transform you. Don't wait until you are gravely ill, with nowhere else to turn, to really understand and know the power of Christ and His grace. C. S. Lewis writes, "Everyone has noticed how hard it is to turn our thought to God when everything is going well with us. . . . We find God an interruption. . . . Or as a friend of mine said, 'We regard God as an airman regards his parachute; it's there for emergencies but he hopes he'll never have to use it.' "[3]

Through daily prayer, soak yourself in God's power and grace moment by moment. Spend time praising and thanking the Lord who heals you (see Exodus 15:26; James 5:13). Pray for the power of Christ's grace to rest upon you, for God's shield to protect the mind, body, and spirit of you and those He brings to your mind. And throughout your days, "Dear friend, I pray that you may enjoy good health and that all may go well with you, even as your soul is getting along well" (3 John 1:2 NIV).

One-Touch Healing

Dear God, I am reaching out my hand to You this morning, knowing that if I can just touch the hem of Your garment, You will make me whole. I envision You before me. I see the compassion in Your eyes. I know that You love me and that nothing is impossible for You. Fill me with Your love. Give me Your healing touch this morning.

For she said within herself, If I may but touch his garment, I shall be whole.

MATTHEW 9:21 KJV

Prayers Offered in Faith

Lord, I am feeling so poorly. You know what is attacking my body. You can see everything. I ask you in prayer, right now, to fill me with Your healing light. Banish the sickness from my body. Fill me with Your presence. Draw me unto You.

Is anyone among you sick? Then he must call for the elders of the church and they are to pray over him, anointing him with oil in the name of the Lord; and the prayer offered in faith will restore the one who is sick.

James 5:14–15 NASB

The Healing Edge

Lord, when I connect with You, when my body is filled with Your power and love, nothing can harm me. I am healed from within. Fill me now with Your presence. Heal my body, soul, and spirit. I praise Your name, for You are the one that heals me, saves me, loves me! Thank You for giving me life!

People. . .begged him to let the sick just touch the edge of his cloak, and all who touched it were healed.

MATTHEW 14:35–36 NIV

Strength in Weakness

It's a paradox, but it is Your truth. When I am weak, I am strong because Your strength is made perfect in my weakness. Because You are in my life, I can rest in You. With Your loving arms around me, I am buoyed in spirit, soul, and body. When I am with You there is peace and comfort.

Therefore I take pleasure in infirmities, in reproaches, in needs, in persecutions, in distresses, for Christ's sake. For when I am weak, then I am strong.

2 Corinthians 12:10 NKJV

Crying Out for Healing

Lord, when Miriam had leprosy, her brother cried out for her healing. I come to You this morning, crying out for You to heal my loved one. She is in so much pain. She needs your comfort, strength, love, and grace. Dear Lord, touch her! Allow her to feel Your presence. Immerse her in Your healing light.

So Moses cried out to the Lord, "Please, God, heal her!"

Numbers 12:13 NIV

His Promise of Restoration

You are the healer of our wounds, the One who restores spirit, soul, and body. Thank You for blessing my life. As I spend this time with You, I feel Your touch upon me. You are my gentle Shepherd, always trying to keep me from harm. Thank You, Jesus, for coming into my life, for making me complete, for restoring me to God. All praise and glory to my Jehova-rapha, the Lord who heals!

For I will restore health to you, and I will heal your wounds, says the Lord.

Jeremiah 30:17 AMP

Relentless Praying

"As he had been doing previously"—what amazing words! Help me to be like Daniel, Lord. When faced with arrest and execution, when all seemed bleak and hopeless, he didn't panic but did as he had always done. He came before You on his knees, giving thanks. Keep me close to You, Lord. Enter my heart as I kneel at Your throne.

[Daniel] *continued kneeling on his knees three times a day, praying and giving thanks before his God, as he had been doing previously.*

DANIEL 6:10 NASB

Healer of Hearts and Wounds

My heart is broken. I no longer have any strength. Fill me with Your power. Put Your arms around me. Let me linger in Your presence, bask in Your love. You are all I need. For without You, I can do nothing. Quench my thirst with Your living water. Feed me with Your bread of life. Nourish me deep within. I come to You in despair. I leave filled with joy.

He heals the brokenhearted and binds up their wounds.

Psalm 147:3 NASB

Looking for His Heart

Here I am, Lord! As you look for those whose hearts are completely Yours, here I am. Look at me, be with me. Support me in this time of need. You know my situation. You know what needs Your healing touch. As I rest silently before You, help me to be still and know You are God. You are my hope, my life, my peace.

"For the eyes of the LORD move to and fro throughout the earth that He may strongly support those whose heart is completely His."

2 CHRONICLES 16:9 NASB

Praise Ye the Lord!

I know that You are the source of all healing. Hold me in the palm of Your hand. Fill my mind, body, and soul with Your presence. I praise You, Lord, for all You have done, are doing, and will do for me! And I praise You for what you are. . .a loving God who is watching over me. Thank You, God. You are so good to me.

Heal me, Lord, and I will be healed;
save me and I will be saved, for you are the one I praise.
Jeremiah 17:14 NIV

All That Is within Me

Everything I am, all that is within me, I draw upon as I praise Your holy name. You have done so many great things and have given me the power to do even greater things as I allow You to live through me. Thank You for healing me, for forgiving me. You are an awesome God!

Bless the Lord, O my soul; and all that is within me, bless His holy name!
Bless the Lord, O my soul, and forget not all His benefits:
who forgives all your iniquities, who heals all your diseases.

Psalm 103:1–3 NKJV

The Power of Confidence in Christ

And they who know Your name [who have experience and acquaintance with Your mercy] will lean on and confidently put their trust in You, for You, Lord, have not forsaken those who seek (inquire of and for) You.

PSALM 9:10 AMP

Fear comes in many sizes, shapes, and forms, from a writer's fear of facing a blank page to a mother's fear of harm coming to her child, we all experience it. When fear invades our spirits, we need to turn to the One in whom we have confidence—Jesus Christ, the Good Shepherd. The One who tells us that He is with us always, "to the very end of the age" (Matthew 28:20 NIV).

The only confidence we have in this life is knowing that God is always with us. He is our Protector, Comforter, and Guide. And if we are wise enough, we will look for and find God in every moment, filled with the assurance that He is with us through the good and the bad, the known and the unknown, the beginning and the end. He is there when others are not. If we follow God—through prayer and the reading and application of His Word—He will keep us close to Him, traveling down the right path, until we reach our home, where He greets us. Within the shelter of His embrace, fear is vanquished.

Be a person with powerful confidence in Christ. Renew your mind each and every morning with God's truth, for that truth is what will keep you confident and expectant throughout the day. Plant God's Word in your heart and mind. Pray for His deliverance: "Deliver me from evil." Leave your fears at His feet.

Reflect on your past experiences, how God has carried you through. Go to your Protector, Guide, and Good Shepherd, for He and His Word are the only things that can set you free from all fear as You trust and hope in Him. Know that "God will command his angels to protect you wherever you go. They will carry you in their arms, and you won't hurt your feet on the stones" (Psalm 91:11–12 CEV).

A Prayer for Deliverance

I am here, seeking You, Lord. I am looking in Your Word for courage and strength. Help me to have more confidence in You. You are my rock and my refuge. Bring me up to where You are. I want to commune with You, to rest with You, to be head over heels "in trust" with You. Show me how to do that, Lord. As I look upon Your face, deliver me from this burden of fear. I long to dwell in Your presence here and now, and when I rise from this place of prayer, I long to take You with me through my day. You are my courage and my strength. Nothing can harm me.

I sought the Lord, and He heard me, and delivered me from all my fears.

Psalm 34:4 NKJV

Never Alone

Your Word says that You will never leave me, but right now I feel all alone. I am afraid of what lies before me. Help me to know, beyond a shadow of a doubt, that You are with me. You are my Good Shepherd. With You by my side, I need not fear. Fill me with Your presence and Your courage as I greet this day.

"I will never leave you nor forsake you."

JOSHUA 1:5 NIV

Calling All Angels

Oh, what a tremendous God You are! You have commanded Your angels to surround me. Right now they are protecting me, guarding me from danger. You will not let anything that is not of Your will touch me. You won't even let me trip over a stone. With Your heavenly host surrounding me, there is no need to fear. Still my rapidly beating heart as I take one breath. . .then another. . .then another, here in Your presence. You are an awesome God. You are my God. Thank You for always being there—here—in my heart.

God will command his angels to protect you wherever you go.
They will carry you in their arms, and you won't hurt your feet on the stones.
Psalm 91:11–12 CEV

Calm My Heart

Lord, rid me of the fears that are plaguing me as I come to You this morning. Calm my racing heart. Fill me with Your strength and courage. The storms, the trials, feel as if they are going to overcome me, but You have overcome the world and will not let me be brought down. You have given me the spirit of power, love, and self-discipline, and I revel in this knowledge. I praise Your name, Your saving name!

God has not given us a spirit of timidity, but of power and love and discipline.

2 Timothy 1:7 NASB

Worldly Fears

I am so blessed for even though I fear many things right now—the state of the economy, unemployment, terrorist attacks, shootings in the schools and on the streets, lack of health care coverage—I trust in You. I refuse to go along with the world, driven by despair, fear, and insecurity. No, I will not bow to outside pressures. I will live my life with the assurance that You are with me. I will put my confidence in You, for I trust You to look out for me, to keep me close to You, to always be with me, no matter what.

"But blessed is the one who trusts in the LORD, whose confidence is in him."

JEREMIAH 17:7 NIV

One Way Out

Lord, I am so afraid of what this day may bring. So many times I have tried to make this situation right and nothing seems to be working. I cannot figure a way out anymore. Help me to trust in You—not just halfway but the whole way. I don't understand what's happening, but I acknowledge Your presence in my life and Your ability to make all things right.

Trust in the Lord with all your heart and lean not on your own understanding; in all your ways submit to him, and he will make your paths straight.

Proverbs 3:5–6 NIV

Fear of the Future

Here I am, Lord, rising before the dawn, crying to You for help for that is the desperate state I am in. I fear what this day may bring, or if not this day, the next. Your Word is the only relief, the only confidence, the only rock on which I can stand. Strengthen me with Your courage. You said You would never leave me nor forsake me. So come to me now. Rise within my spirit. Lift me up to the Rock that is higher than I. I want to soar like an eagle and fly into Your arms where I know I will be safe, protected, and loved. Keep Your hand upon me this day and all my days.

I rise early, before the sun is up; I cry out for help and put my hope in your words.

PSALM 119:147 NLT

In God I Trust

When all is said and done, it simply comes down to this, Lord: In whom do I trust? If I allow messages from the devil to fill my mind, I will be defeated. You have overcome this world, You have overcome the evil one. Plant Your Word in my mind so that there is no room for the fears that threaten to consume me. Help me to remember that I need never fear, for You are with me.

But even when I am afraid, I keep on trusting you. I praise your promises! I trust you and am not afraid. No one can harm me.

Psalm 56:3–4 CEV

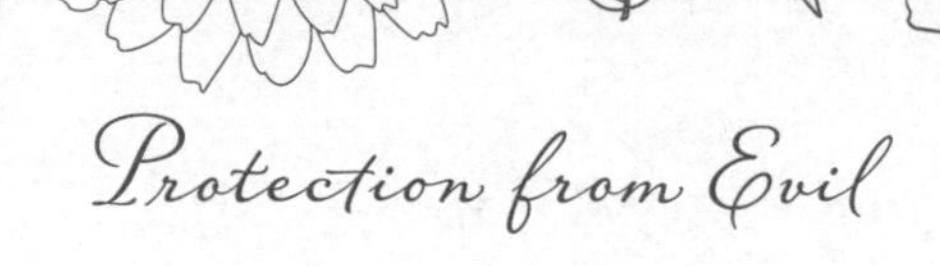

Protection from Evil

It is well with my soul, for I am Your child and You protect me from all evils. I come to You, pouring out my heart, sharing my fears and worries. Take these fears from me and shepherd me to a place close beside You. Snuggle up close to me and fill me with the comfort of Your Word. Help me to be still and listen to Your advice. I want to know what You want me to do. Dispel the negative thoughts and fill me with Your Word, for that is the power that will get me through this day and the days to come.

My victory and honor come from God alone. He is my refuge, a rock where no enemy can reach me. O my people, trust in him at all times. Pour out your heart to him, for God is our refuge.

Psalm 62:7–8 NLT

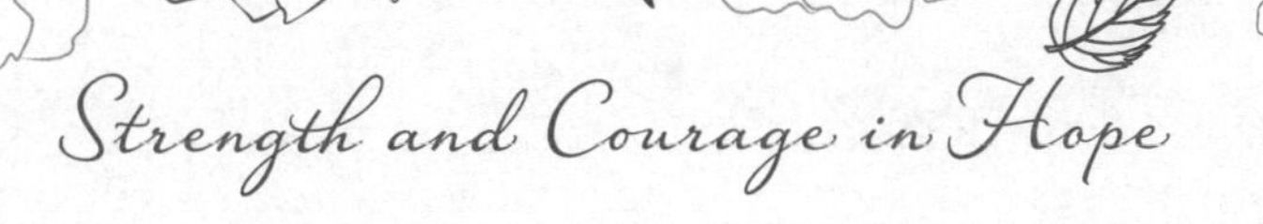

Strength and Courage in Hope

Each and every day, just like today, I arise in the morning, afraid of what the day may bring. But then I remember You, and I come to You in prayer. Your Word brings me light. Your presence brings me comfort. I breathe in Your strength and exhale my fears. Strength in. . .fears out. I have courage of spirit and strength of heart for all my hope—today and every day—is in You and You alone.

Be of good courage, and He shall strengthen your heart,
all you who hope in the Lord.
Psalm 31:24 NKJV

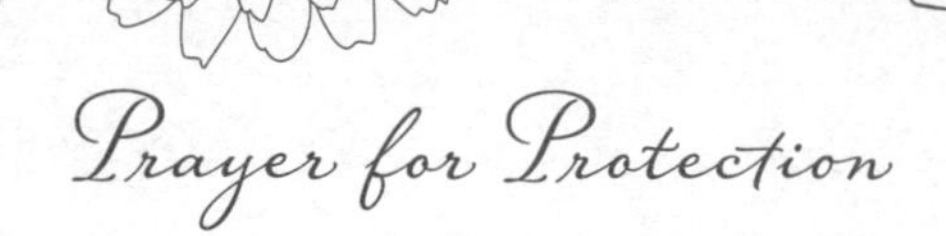

Prayer for Protection

Lord, help me to be a frugal Christian and not throw away my confidence in You. Fill my spirit with power and courage so I can face this day with You beside me, ready to protect me at a moment's notice. I believe in You. You will save me, bringing me through the fire and flood, the storm and desert. You are holding my hand, shielding me from the evils of this world. Thank You, Lord, for walking with me through the shadows of this valley.

So do not throw away your confidence; it will be richly rewarded. . . .
But we do not belong to those who shrink back and are destroyed,
but of those who have faith and are saved.

HEBREWS 10:35, 39 NIV

The Power of Walking with God

It is God who works in you both to will and to do for His good pleasure.
PHILIPPIANS 2:13 NKJV

We are called to "*Be* still, and know that I am God" (Psalm 46:10 NKJV, emphasis added). But when we are caught up in society's frenzied pace, our seemingly endless to-do list threatens to crowd out our time "to be"—with God, our spouse, our children, our friends. So how do we decide every day what God wants us to do? And how can we prevent our frantic quest of *doing* from stealing our joy of *being*?

First, every morning go to God for renewal and edification. He will give you the energy to do whatever needs to be done. "He energizes those who get tired. . . . Those who wait upon god get fresh strength" (Isaiah 40:29, 31 THE MESSAGE). And as He is refreshing and energizing you, He's listening. Present your to-do lists for His input. Allow God to reorient your priorities in light of Romans 12:2—"Don't be like the people of this world, but let God change the way you think. Then you will know how *to do* everything that is good and pleasing to him" (CEV, emphasis added).

Second, realize your limits. You may not get everything done in one day. Take a look at the tasks listed and, if necessary, pare them down to a manageable number. Sometimes it's necessary to allow others to help share the load you bear. John Wesley said, "Though I am always in haste, I am never in a hurry, because I never undertake more work than I can go through with calmness of spirit." Ask God for guidance in what not "to do."

Third, spend time *being* as you're *doing*. Throughout the activities of your day, be the child God wants you to be, one filled with love and joy, one who is patient, forgiving, and kind, calm, unhurried, anxious about nothing. Take time to smell the coffee, to look around at God's wonders, to just *be*.

Overwhelmed

God, I have so many things to do today. I feel overwhelmed. But I am here to be Your hands and feet. You have known since the beginning of time what I am to accomplish each and every day. Give me the wisdom to do what You want me to do, to be the person You want me to be.

For we are His workmanship, created in Christ Jesus for good works, which God prepared beforehand that we should walk in them.

EPHESIANS 2:10 NKJV

Renew My Strength

I didn't get half the things I needed to do accomplished yesterday, Lord. And today I feel as if I have no energy. I am flagging, Lord, and I don't know what to do. So I arise early and come here to spend time with You. Calm my nerves. Remind me that the world is not going to fall apart if I don't accomplish everything on my to-do list today or even tomorrow, yet show me how to use my time wisely. Give my heart peace, and as I spend these moments with You, give me strength so that I may walk in Your power.

He gives power to the weak, and to those who have no might He increases strength. . . . Those who wait on the Lord *shall renew their strength; they shall mount up with wings like eagles, they shall run and not be weary, they shall walk and not faint.*

Isaiah 40:29, 31 NKJV

Let It Be

I acknowledge that You are in control of everything, Lord, and that the things You want me to accomplish today will get done. I want to walk in Your will and not in mine. I want to lean on Your Word and take Your paths. I can only do that by putting my total trust in You as I go through this day. I want to be like Mary. I want to be Your servant, saying, " 'Let it be to me according to your word' " (Luke 1:38 NKJV). So, Lord, help me to accomplish want You want me to do today, and let the rest be.

Trust in the Lord with all your heart, and lean not on your own understanding; in all your ways acknowledge Him, and He shall direct your paths.

Proverbs 3:5–6 NKJV

Change My Thoughts

Lord, I don't want to be like the people of this world, running around at breakneck speed, trying to multitask until I'm so deep in the darkness I can no longer see the light of Your face. It's not all about doing; it's about being. Change my way of thinking to Your way of thinking. I take this to-do list and place it in Your capable hands. Help me to see this list through Your eyes. Show me clearly the steps I am to take today.

Don't be like the people of this world, but let God change the way you think. Then you will know how to do everything that is good and pleasing to him.

ROMANS 12:2 CEV

Rush Hour

Here I am, Lord, getting ready for another busy day, preparing myself to face rush hour. Help me to stay calm throughout this day and not get caught up in the frenzied pace of this world but to set a pace that is pleasing to You. Sure and steady wins the race, and my race is to win the prize of Your presence in my life. Help me to keep that in the forefront of my mind today. May I not become anxious but keep Your Word of peace in my heart and be a beacon of peace in the presence of others.

Anxiety in the heart of man causes depression, but a good word makes it glad.

PROVERBS 12:25 NKJV

My Main Desire

Lord, help me to keep the main thing the main thing—and that is to seek first the kingdom of God, beholding Your beauty, inquiring in Your temple. That is all that is truly important, not whether or not I get all my work done at home, the office, or church. As I receive requests for my time and ability, give me wisdom to say yes and no in accordance with Your will.

One thing I have desired of the Lord, that will I seek: That I may dwell in the house of the Lord all the days of my life, to behold the beauty of the Lord, and to inquire in His temple.

Psalm 27:4 NKJV

Priorities

Lord, as I go through this day, help me to keep my priorities straight. It's not all about what I do but how I treat others. Show me how to love those I come in contact with as I go through my daily routine and run my errands. Help me be a person of compassion. When people see me, I want them to recognize You, because that's what the world needs more of these days—Your love, Your face, Your presence, Your light.

"God is with you in all that you do."

GENESIS 21:22 NKJV

Capturing Thoughts

God, it seems like I need a reminder every moment of the day to listen to Your voice. I keep getting caught up in the world of busyness and that's not where You want me to be. Help me not to be overwhelmed by the demands of this society but to be open to Your voice. I want to hear You speak to me all throughout the day. I want to do only what You want me to do each moment. Remind me to take each thought captive to Christ so that I am not misled, going somewhere or doing something that is not of You.

We are taking every thought captive to the obedience of Christ.

2 Corinthians 10:5 nasb

No Worries

I'm not letting the worries of this day get me away from You, Lord. I'll not go out into the world seeking gold—a temporary blessing at best—but You and Your will. I seek first Your presence as I come to You in prayer. I lay myself before You, Your willing servant. May everything I do today leave Your fingerprints, because that is why You created me. Help me to be a blessing to all those I meet.

"The seed which fell among the thorns, these are the ones who have heard, and as they go on their way they are choked with worries and riches and pleasures of this life, and bring no fruit to maturity."

LUKE 8:14 NASB

Peace amid Interruptions

Here I am, Lord, ready to receive my marching orders for today. Arm me with faith, love, and hope. I am strong in You. I expect You to be with me all through the day. There is nothing that can frustrate me when I remain in Your presence. With every interruption, I am calm and accepting, because the prince of this world, the evil one, is unable to steal my peace and joy. For You, my Lord and Savior, have overcome this world! Hallelujah!

We continually remember before our God and Father your work produced by faith, your labor prompted by love, and your endurance inspired by hope in our Lord Jesus Christ.

1 THESSALONIANS 1:3 NIV

God's Glory, not Mine

It's all for You, Lord, everything I do today. I refuse to get caught up in the mad rush. I refuse to seek only temporal satisfaction. I am here to please You and You only. Help me not to stretch myself so thin that I am unable to do the things You want me to do. I am here for You and for You alone. Give me the energy I need to accomplish those tasks for Your glory. And tonight may You say, "Ah, my good and faithful servant, well done!"

Whatever you do, do all to the glory of God.

1 CORINTHIANS 10:31 NASB

The Power of Assurance

I will bless you [with abundant increase of favors]. . .
and you will be a blessing [dispensing good to others].
GENESIS 12:2 AMP

Is your faith strong enough and your mind open enough to make room for God's bounty of blessings? Or is your faith too little, your mind too closed? Perhaps you feel you are undeserving. If so, plant the words of Hebrews 11:6 in your heart: "Without faith it is impossible to please and be satisfactory to Him. For whoever would come near to God must [necessarily] believe that God exists and that He is the rewarder of those who earnestly and diligently seek Him [out]" (AMP). Claim the promise of 1 John 5:14–15: "Now this is the confidence that we have in Him, that if we ask anything according to His will, He hears us. And if we know that He hears us, whatever we ask, we know that we have the petitions that we have asked of Him" (NKJV). It's not a matter of deserving but of firm faith, great expectation, and sincere seeking.

Go to God and ask Him to plant a seed in your mind, giving you specific ways to bless others in specific instances. Spend some quiet moments in His presence, listening for His direction. Then make sure you do what He tells you. For a general idea of how to be a blessing to everyone, consider 1 Peter 3:10–12: "Whoever wants to embrace life and see the day fill up with good, here's what you do: Say nothing evil or hurtful; snub evil and cultivate good; run after peace for all you're worth. God looks on all this with approval, listening and responding well to what he's asked" (THE MESSAGE).

Empty yourself of disbelief and discouragement. Revel in the power of assurance that God is ready and willing to bless your life. Choose to believe that Christ loves you and is blessing you even in the midst of trials. He always goes before you, planting blessings on your path. God is One who "daily loads us with benefits" (Psalm 68:19 NKJV). Your job: Claim them today.

Sharing My Blessings

Lord, You have blessed me and the works of my hands. I am so grateful to You for all that I have. As You bless me, I am able to bless others in whatever way I can. What a feeling to know that I am able to help expand Your kingdom! Help me to tithe my talents, monies, and time, all to Your glory. For Thine is the kingdom and the power, forever and ever.

"Every man shall give as he is able, according to the blessing of the Lord your God which He has given you."

Deuteronomy 16:17 NASB

Obedience and Blessings

I hear Your voice, Lord, and I thank You for the blessings that You have showered upon me. Sometimes I feel so unworthy, but You love me so much that at times I cannot understand it. All that You have blessed me with goes beyond me, as I respond to Your voice, do Your will, and work to serve others. Speak to me, Lord. Tell me whom, what, and where You want me to bless. I am Your servant, Lord; speak to me.

All these blessings will come down on you and spread out beyond you because you have responded to the Voice of God, your God.

Deuteronomy 28:2 MSG

Guaranteed Blessing

Your Word says that You actually guarantee a blessing on everything I do! That's a promise I can count on, and one I delight in. It gives me the confidence that You will be with me in all that I do, blessing me at each and every turn. What an awesome promise! I arise today, assured of Your assistance, guidance, and approval of every good thing. There are no words to express how You make me feel. I am humbled in Your presence and renewed in Your light. I praise You, Lord!

"The Lord will guarantee a blessing on everything you do."

Deuteronomy 28:8 NLT

Choosing Life

Lord, this day I choose life—I choose to live and work and have my being in You. Instead of looking at all that I don't have, I choose to look at all that You have blessed me with—family, friends, a home, a job, clothes on my back, food in my belly. . . . Oh Lord, the list is endless. Thank You so much for being my life, today and every day! I cling to You, each and every moment. Live through me!

"I call heaven and earth as witnesses today against you, that I have set before you life and death, blessing and cursing; therefore choose life, that both you and your descendants may live."

DEUTERONOMY 30:19 NKJV

An Awesome God

It is Your presence, Your blessings, Your love that makes my life so rich and fulfilling. I am not worried about what others have and I have not. I am full of joy for what I do have—mainly You! There is nothing greater than You, Lord. You are an awesome God. Nothing I do can make You any greater than Your Word and Your promises. I praise You for what You are doing in my life, for making me rich beyond my wildest dreams as I live and breathe in You.

God's blessing makes life rich; nothing we do can improve on God.

Proverbs 10:22 MSG

Daily Benefits

I am loaded with benefits! Blessed beyond compare! You, the God of my salvation, the Friend who laid down His life for me, the One who is with me in fire, flood, and famine, the One who will never leave me or forsake me! Today is a new day, and You have benefits waiting out there for me. I begin the day in my walk toward You, leaving my burdens behind and focusing on the benefits ahead. And when I come to You at the close of the day, You will be waiting for me, at the end of the path, with a good word.

Blessed be the Lord, who daily loads us with benefits, the God of our salvation!

PSALM 68:19 NKJV

The Right Focus

Lord, I am thirsty, parched with the demands of this world. I am in want in so many ways. Help me not to focus on what I don't have, but to focus on You and the blessings that You have prepared for me and my children. Pour out Your Spirit upon me now. Fill me with Your presence. Give me hope for this day. I anticipate blessings waiting around every corner. Thank You, Lord, for taking such good care of me. You, my Savior, are the greatest blessing of all!

"For I will pour out water to quench your thirst and to irrigate your parched fields. And I will pour out my Spirit on your descendants, and my blessing on your children."

Isaiah 44:3 NLT

A Symbol and Source of Blessing

Lord, Your Son has already rescued me! I am so full of joy! You have made me both a symbol of that blessing and a source of blessing to others. I am not afraid of things in this world for I am assured of Your promises. I will be strong, confident in the benefits You bestow upon me, able to stretch myself as I strive to reach others so that they, too, will have the benefit of Your blessings. What power! What confidence! What hope!

"Now I will rescue you and make you both a symbol and a source of blessing. So don't be afraid. Be strong."

ZECHARIAH 8:13 NLT

Sowing and Reaping

Lord, Your Word says it is true—the more I give, the more I get. Yet that's not why I do it. I give of myself to bless others because that is what You have called me to do. The more I step out in Your Word, with You walking before me, the more I am blessed by Your presence and Your promises. It's not all about material things, although those are blessings as well. But I am more focused on the spiritual, for that is what keeps me close to You, unshaken, undisturbed, unfettered. Praise be Your holy name!

"Bring your full tithe to the Temple treasury so there will be ample provisions in my Temple. Test me in this and see if I don't open up heaven itself to you and pour out blessings beyond your wildest dreams."

MALACHI 3:10 MSG

Heavenly Blessings

Because I am united with Your Son, who gave His life so that we could live, You have blessed me with every spiritual blessing. Here I sit, at my Savior's knee, His hand upon my head. I am at peace. I am blessed. I am in the heavenly realms. Here, nothing can harm me, for He has blessed me beyond measure. Lord, my cup runneth over with love for You!

All praise to God, the Father of our Lord Jesus Christ, who has blessed us with every spiritual blessing in the heavenly realms because we are united with Christ.

EPHESIANS 1:3 NLT

A Daily Benediction

May You walk down the road with me today. May You shower my path with Your many blessings. May You keep me from danger. May Your light keep me from the darkness surrounding me. May You give me grace and peace and strength for the day. May You give me someone to bless as You have blessed me. May You be there, waiting for me, at the end of the day, with a good word to calm my spirit as I rest in Your arms.

"'The Lord bless you, and keep you; the Lord make His face shine on you, and be gracious to you; the Lord lift up His countenance on you, and give you peace.'"

Numbers 6:24–26 NASB

The Power of Contentment

True godliness with contentment is itself great wealth.
1 TIMOTHY 6:6 NLT

God wants us to be content—physically, emotionally, and financially—no matter what our circumstances. Money in itself is not evil. Our Creator wants us to prosper. He just doesn't want affluence to obscure our vision of living godly lives. He knows that the more we have materially, the less we will perceive a need for Him (see Deuteronomy 8:1–18). So, to prevent money and finances from being the main focus of our lives, several things must be kept in mind.

First and foremost, we are to seek God and His righteousness (see Matthew 6:33). It's okay to want to have enough money to provide for you and yours and maybe a little extra for that dream vacation. In fact, we are called to be diligent in taking care of ourselves and our family (see 1 Timothy 5:8). The problems arise when we begin loving money for itself, for *that* is the root of all evil (see 1 Timothy 6:10 KJV). Jesus said, "Ye cannot serve God and mammon" (Matthew 6:24 KJV). Make serving and worshiping the Lord your number one priority.

Second, we are to be wise in the spending of money. Our constant pursuit of the latest gadget can easily lead us into debt and perhaps financial ruin. We need to guard against the plethora of advertising ploys out there. Ask yourself and God, "Is this item truly necessary?"

Third, we are to be content with what we have. This truism is covered not only in 1 Timothy 6:6 but also in two of the Ten Commandments, where God tells us neither to steal nor to covet our neighbor's possessions (see Exodus 20:15, 17). When we find ourselves discontent with what we have, we are "greedy for gain," which "takes away the life of its owners" (Proverbs 1:19 NKJV).

Finally, we cannot allow money worries to steal our joy. Remember the words of Jesus, who told us to be anxious for nothing (see Matthew 6:25–32). Rest in the assurance that God cares about us and will see to our every need.

Learned Contentment

Lord, I am so happy just as I am. There is nothing better than being in Your presence, seeking Your face. I thank You for all my blessings, in good times and bad. I thank You for Your Son, who died on the cross so that I could live forever. I thank You for Your Word and the treasures I find there. I go forth in this day, with the power of contentment firmly in my heart. Lead me where You will. I am ready to follow.

I have learned, in whatsoever state I am, therewith to be content.

Philippians 4:11 KJV

Strength for the Work Ahead

You promised to bless me and mine. I thank You for all the spiritual, physical, and financial gifts You have showered upon me. You give me the physical strength to go out each and every day to work and support myself and my family. Your Word gives me the spiritual strength to battle the schemes that the evil one throws into my path. Thank You for hearing my prayers, morning after morning, strengthening me for the work ahead.

If you start thinking to yourselves, "I did all this. And all by myself. I'm rich. It's all mine!"—well, think again. Remember that God, your God, gave you the strength to produce all this wealth so as to confirm the covenant that he promised to your ancestors—as it is today.

Deuteronomy 8:18 MSG

Steady Work

Lord, show me how to be content with my job. I know I need to work diligently so that I can provide for my family but I am not sure that this is what You have called me to do. I feel trapped. Would chasing after my dream job be Your will for me or is it just a whim? Lead me in the way I should go. Help me to be content in my present job and with the money I am earning. But if it be Your will, give me the courage to pursue the dreams You have for me.

The one who stays on the job has food on the table;
the witless chase whims and fancies.
PROVERBS 12:11 MSG

Firstfruits for God

Another paycheck! Thank You, God, for giving me the strength to work each day. Thank You for the money I hold in my hand. Help me to remember that this is not my money, but Yours. I come to You this morning, asking You to tell me how much You want me to give to You and, if so directed, others. I want to bless Your church, Your ministries, Your people, as You have so richly blessed me. Tell me, Lord, what You would have me give away, and I will do so knowing that You will bless me.

Honor the Lord with your wealth and with the firstfruits of all your produce; then your barns will be filled with plenty, and your vats will be bursting with wine.

Proverbs 3:9–10 ESV

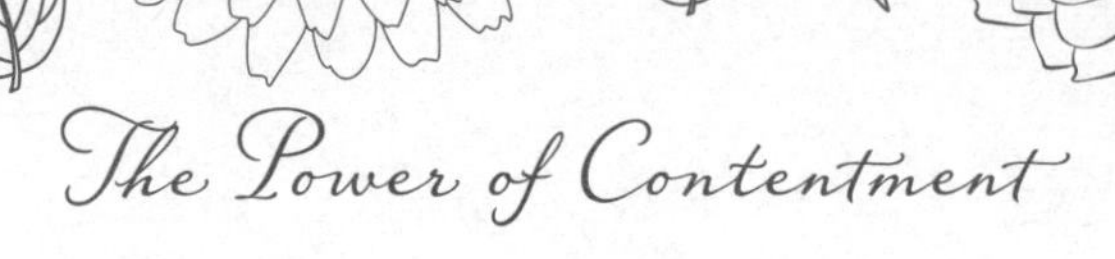

The Power of Contentment

Oh Lord, I feel as if I have it all. With You in my life, I need not worry about anything. For as You dress the flowers that neither toil nor spin and feed the birds that neither sow nor reap, You shall do even more for me. I do not worry about what I will eat, wear, drink, or earn today. I leave all my concerns in Your hands, knowing that You will provide. You are first in my life.

But godliness with contentment is great gain. For we brought nothing into this world, and it is certain we can carry nothing out. And having food and raiment let us be therewith content.

1 Timothy 6:6–8 KJV

Love of Money

Dear God, I come to You this morning with a heavy heart. I feel as if I have let my quest for financial security take my eyes off of You. Help me to put aside my fear of never having enough and replace it with trust in You. Take away my seemingly insatiable appetite for more and more gain and replace it with the power of contentment. Free me from the snare of greed and lead me to greater faith.

For the love of money is the root of all evil: which while some coveted after, they have erred from the faith, and pierced themselves through with many sorrows. But thou, O man of God, flee these things; and follow after righteousness, godliness, faith, love, patience, meekness.

1 Timothy 6:10–11 KJV

Hope in God

I am setting my hope on You this morning, Lord, for You provide me with everything to enjoy. Your treasure of creation—trees, flowers, children, animals, sunsets, stars—are wonders to my eyes and a balm to my heart. With You supplying all that I need, I can do good works, be ready to share, and thus build up treasures in heaven. This way of life, enveloped by Your presence, is the true way. Keep my feet sure on this path. Take care of me today and through the days to come.

As for the rich in this present age, charge them not to be haughty, nor to set their hopes on the uncertainty of riches, but on God, who richly provides us with everything to enjoy. They are to do good, to be rich in good works, to be generous and ready to share, thus storing up treasure for themselves as a good foundation for the future, so that they may take hold of that which is truly life.

1 Timothy 6:17–19 ESV

Trusting in the Lord

Lord, it is You that I trust. Not these things surrounding me, the possessions that money can buy. Those things are not alive. They are not eternal. They will never save me. Only You can do that. And when I die, these earthly things will no longer exist in my world because I will be with You in the eternal heavenlies. Thus, I will spend my life trusting in and focusing on You, knowing that You, my Good Shepherd, will take care of me, supplying all I need and more.

Blessed is the man that trusteth in the Lord, and whose hope the Lord is.

Jeremiah 17:7 KJV

The True Owner

All I have is Yours. My spouse, my children, my parents, my car, my house, my furniture—everything is Yours. Whew! Somehow that takes a load off of my mind, knowing that I am merely Your steward. Give me the wisdom, Lord, to use the things of which You have given me temporary custody to further Your kingdom. I want to live my life to Your glory, not mine. Help me to do that today. Speak to my heart, I pray.

"The earth and everything in it belong to the Lord."

1 Corinthians 10:26 CEV

The Right Heartset

A heartset is like a mindset, Lord. Each morning I need to ask myself where my heart is. Is it set on making lots of money so that I can buy things I don't really need? Is my heart set on showing how much better off I am than my neighbor? Rather, I pray that my heart is set on You and what You want me to do each and every moment of the day. Help me not get caught up in this "me" world. I want my life to be all about You.

"Did I set my heart on making big money or worship at the bank? Did I boast about my wealth, show off because I was well-off? . . . If so, I would deserve the worst of punishments, for I would be betraying God himself."

Job 31:24–25, 28 MSG

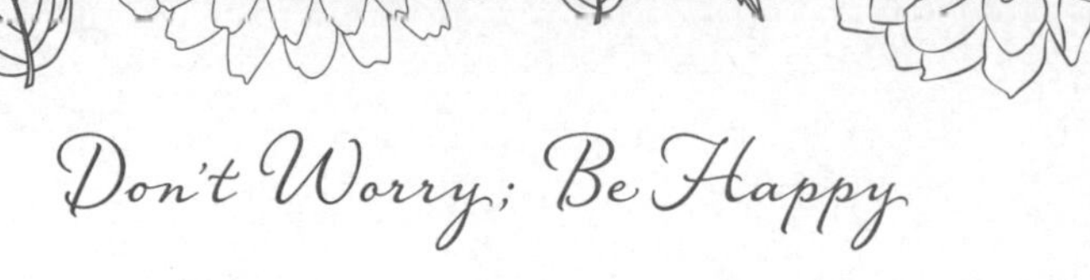

Don't Worry; Be Happy

Your Word says I'm not to worry about my life but that seems to be all that I do. I wonder how I'm going to pay all these bills. How did I get into such a mess? Get me back on the right track, Lord. Help me to get out of debt and stay out. Help me to not worry about where the next dollar is coming from but to put all my trust in You. You know all that I need. Please, Lord, provide for me and mine.

"For this reason I say to you, do not be worried about your life, as to what you will eat or what you will drink; nor for your body, as to what you will put on. . . . For your heavenly Father knows that you need all these things."

MATTHEW 6:25, 32 NASB

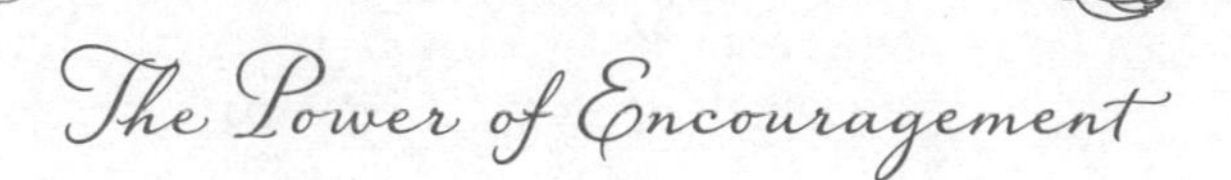

The Power of Encouragement

"But my mouth would encourage you;
comfort from my lips would bring you relief."
Job 16:5 NIV

The truest earthly friends are those who share their faith in our heavenly Father. The best biblical example of friendship is that of David and Jonathan. Even though his father, King Saul, seemed determined to kill David, Jonathan told his friend, "Whatsoever thy soul desireth, I will even do it for thee" (1 Samuel 20:4 KJV). In 1 Samuel 18, we read that Jonathan "loved [David] as he loved his own soul" (verse 3 KJV; see also 1 Samuel 20:17). Also in 1 Samuel, Jonathan made covenants with David (see 18:3; 20:8, 16) as well as informed him of danger (see 19:2); interceded for him (see 19:3); reconciled him to another (see 19:3–7); wept with him (see 20:41); helped to rescue him (see 20:12–13); prayed for him (see 20:13); appealed to God for him (see 20:23); and bound him to himself with promises (see 20:14–16).

At their last encounter, "Jonathan. . .went to David into the wood, and strengthened his hand in God. And he said unto him, Fear not: for the hand of Saul my father shall not find thee; and thou shalt be king over Israel, and I shall be next unto thee; and that also Saul my father knoweth. And they two made a covenant before the Lord" (1 Samuel 23:16–18 KJV). What a friendship!

Each and every day, make it a point to encourage your friends through prayer, comfort, service, listening, and blessings. But most of all, love them, as Jonathan loved David, as Jesus loves us.

Tap into the power of encouragement and love from the greatest resource at our disposal, our greatest Friend—our one and only Savior, Jesus Christ (see John 15:15). He will never leave us nor forsake us (see Hebrews 13:5). How can He when He lives within our hearts?

Consistent Love

All I need is love! That's all I need from my friends right now. People who care about me, who want what's best for me, who will never turn away. But when I look at my past, I wonder if I've always loved my friends. I mean that constant, undying, unyielding love, the kind that You show for us. Forgive me, Lord, for the times I have fallen short. For times that I was so caught up in the busyness of my day that I did not show love to a friend who really needed it. Lord, fill me and my friends with Your love, and help us to let it flow freely to all we meet.

A friend loveth at all times.

Proverbs 17:17 KJV

Love One Another

What an example of love You give us, Jesus! You laid down Your life for everyone—even while we were still sinners. Fill me with that kind of love, Lord, that self-sacrificing love. So often, my thoughts seem to be all about me and what I want. Help me to change that by following Your example. I want to be like You, serving others with compassion, understanding, patience, and kindness. Give me that power, that longing, to love those who love me, those who hate me, and those who are indifferent to me.

[Jesus said], *Love one another; as I have loved you.*

JOHN 13:34 KJV

Turning the Other Cheek

Job prayed for his friends even though they had showed him their true colors. That's a true friend, Lord. And when he did this, You blessed him, giving him twice as much as he had before. That's the true power of forgiveness. You know the relationships I have with my friends. Sometimes it's hard to overlook the hurtful things they say and do. Help me to be more like Job—to learn to turn the other cheek and actually serve friends who disappoint me. I ask for that kind of compassion and dedication to my friends, Lord.

The Lord restored the fortunes of Job when he prayed for his friends, and the Lord increased all that Job had twofold.

Job 42:10 NASB

Loyalty

Lord, I want to be a better friend to those I love. Help me to be trustworthy, devoted, and reliable. Help me to put the desires of my friends before my own. Give me the power of encouragement, so that I may be at their side with a ready word and a shoulder to lean on, with love in my heart and a prayer on my lips. I want to be like Jonathan was for David. I want to clothe others with the warmth of friendship. Make me a true friend. Whom can I help today?

"Is this your loyalty to your friend? Why did you not go with your friend?"

2 Samuel 16:17 NASB

Weeping with Friends

Lord, my friend is in distress. She has lost something very dear to her and she has sunk down into the abyss. Give me the power of encouragement so that I can help bear her burden. She has been there for me so many times. Now I'd like to repay that kindness, that love that she has given to me. Ease my schedule so that I can take the time out of my day to give her words of comfort. Help me lift her to You.

"But first, please let me spend two months, wandering in the hill country with my friends. We will cry together."

JUDGES 11:37 CEV

Forgiving Love

You are love and You came into the world to show us that love. When we love others, we are doing what You have called us to do. But right now, Lord, I need help swallowing the resentment I feel toward my friend. She has betrayed me, and I don't know how I can love her again without Your help. This morning I pray for that forgiving love. I am saved, born of You, and I know You. Now I ask for Your love to fill me to overflowing. Help me to forgive. Heal my wounds, O Lord, my strength and song.

Beloved, let us love one another: for love is of God;
and every one that loveth is born of God, and knoweth God.
1 John 4:7 KJV

The Kindness of Friends

Lord, after being through this time of trial, I understand who my true friends are. Some have turned away from me, some have become indifferent to me, some no longer seek my companionship. I cannot lie. They have disappointed me. But I have also been blessed with kind friends who stick with me through thick and thin, friends who have modeled You in their lives. Thank You for those friends. May I prove myself worthy of such loyalty. And thank You, Lord, for Your eternal forgiveness and friendship. You are the One I praise!

"For the despairing man there should be kindness from his friend; so that he does not forsake the fear of the Almighty."

Job 6:14 NASB

The Help of Intercessors

I can't stop crying, Lord. So much has happened. Give me the courage to call friends, asking them to pray for me. I need their strength and encouragement. I feel so alone. I need them to help me through this, but that makes me feel weak. Yet Your Word tells me that when I am weak, You are strong. Help me to put my self-reliance aside as I seek the comfort and intercession of others. Give me courage to humble myself as I draw closer to You this morning.

"My intercessor is my friend as my eyes pour out tears to God."

JOB 16:20 NIV

Blessed with Friends

There are many wonderful things in this life, Lord. The smell of a baby's breath, the touch of a warm hand, the taste of dark chocolate—but a good word, deed, or thought from a friend is even better. There are times when I am so down. And then a friend blesses me and I think of You. It's because of You and the love that You give that makes us want to reach out to others. Thank You for blessing my life with friends.

The sweet smell of incense can make you feel good, but true friendship is better still.

Proverbs 27:9 CEV

Sacrificial Love

What a sacrifice—to lay down one's life for another! Yet that is exactly what You did for us. You allowed Yourself to be crucified and then asked God to forgive us for that dastardly deed. Oh, what a burden You bore for us. Allow me to repay You in some small way by laying my life down for my own friends. Give me the attitude of a servant, a servant like You, Jesus. Whom can I pray for and encourage today?

Greater love hath no man than this, that a man lay down his life for his friends.

John 15:13 KJV

Servant Love

O Lord, I want to do whatever my friends desire, as long as it is in accordance with Your Word. May I have the same attitude with my friends as Jonathan had with David. He served him so well, doing whatever David's soul desired. That is servant love, the kind You continually show us. Help me to be a better friend. Let me know what to say, when to speak, and whom to encourage. I want to do Your will in the world. Lead me on!

[Jonathan said to David,] *Whatsoever thy soul desireth, I will even do it for thee.*

1 Samuel 20:4 KJV

The Power of Rest and Refreshment

Come to Me, all you who labor and are heavy-laden and overburdened, and I will cause you to rest. [I will ease and relieve and refresh your souls.]
MATTHEW 11:28 AMP

Stress is nothing new. Since Adam and Eve, people have always been under some sort of pressure—but it's important to understand that stress today is linked to such health problems as cancer, heart disease, accidental injuries, suicide, and depression. What can we do to protect ourselves against stress, to shore up our foundation of trust in God, so that our true character will be a consistent and overwhelming peace of Christ—within and without?

The first protective measure against stress is to make sure we take a weekly Sabbath rest. Spend time in His presence, reading God's Word and Christian literature. Feed your mind as you rest your body.

Second, focus on and trust in God. In times of anxiety, we tend to let fear replace faith. Constantly remind yourself that with Jesus, you have nothing to fear. You can trust in the One who will never leave you nor forsake you. Keep your eye on Christ, not your fears or circumstances.

Third, daily ask God to help you keep your peace and give you joy on the journey through life, knowing that stress, although tortuous at times, *can* make you a stronger person (see James 1:2–4). All the while keep in mind that no matter how difficult a situation may seem, nothing is impossible with God.

Finally, give your burdens to Jesus and leave them there. His shoulders were made to carry them. " 'Come to Me, all you who labor and are heavy laden, and I will give you rest' " (Matthew 11:28 NKJV).

On Eagles' Wings

God, I need You to lift me up, above all these problems, above my circumstances, above my helplessness. Carry me off to Your place in the heavenlies, where I can find my breath, where I can sit with You, where I can find the peace of Your presence. You alone can carry me through this. I feel myself drifting off, Your strong arms holding me close, Your breath touching my face. Thank You, Lord, for saving my soul. My spirit rejoices!

"I carried you on eagles' wings and brought you to myself."

Exodus 19:4 NIV

Needing Direction

Lord, I come before You, standing here, seeking Your face. I need direction. I feel so lost, so alone. But You are here with me, to lead and to guide me, to show me the way I should go. With You and You alone, I can find rest for my soul. Give me the peace of Jesus. Peace like a river. Peace. . . Peace. . . Peace. . . Lord, give me peace.

Thus says the Lord: "Stand in the ways and see, and ask for the old paths, where the good way is, and walk in it; then you will find rest for your souls."

Jeremiah 6:16 NKJV

Running to God

I have been running, running, running in all different directions, but I need to run to You now and stay here in Your presence. I am thirsting for You as I have never thirsted before. My future looks bleak. I cannot see beyond my troubles. But I now focus on Your light. It warms my skin, touches my heart, and speaks to my soul. I join my spirit with Yours and rest here at Your feet.

As the deer pants for the water brooks, so my soul pants for You, O God. My soul thirsts for God, for the living God.

Psalm 42:1–2 NASB

Pile It on Jesus

Lord, my burdens are so heavy. My bones hurt from all the pressure. With each breath I take, I draw myself closer to You. With each beat of my heart, I am nearer to Your peace. Touch my body, Lord, and my heart and soul. My spirit wants to cling to You for strength, love, and compassion. Take away the hurt and fill me with Your strength. Help me to relax in Your presence. Give me a good word from Your lips. Take the burdens from me. Help me to leave them at Your feet.

Pile your troubles on God's shoulders—he'll carry your load, he'll help you out. He'll never let good people topple into ruin. . . . I trust in [God].

Psalm 55:22–23 MSG

Lifted out of the Pit

I am in such turmoil. I don't understand what's happening or why. All I know is that I am stressed out and I can't seem to get a handle on anything anymore. Lift me up out of this pit, Lord. I trust in You. I know that You can uphold me, that You can help me rise above my troubles, for You have overcome this world. I know that I am precious in Your sight and You will not allow evil to harm me. Save me, lift me, meet me now!

"'Do not fear, for I am with you; do not anxiously look about you,
for I am your God. I will strengthen you, surely I will help you,
surely I will uphold you with My righteous right hand.'"

Isaiah 41:10 NASB

True Colors

Lord, I haven't been handling the stress very well lately. How do I let myself get into these situations? I know I am to consider it a challenge when I am under pressure, but right now I feel like I'm challenged out. Help me to find joy in the journey, Lord. To remember that no matter what happens, You are on this ride with me. May the pressure that is on me now make me more like Christ. Lord, I pray for Your peace!

Consider it a sheer gift, friends, when tests and challenges come at you from all sides. You know that under pressure, your faith-life is forced into the open and shows its true colors. So don't try to get out of anything prematurely. Let it do its work so you become mature and well-developed, not deficient in any way.

James 1:2–4 MSG

Days of Trouble

Everywhere I go, everywhere I look—at home, the office, the world—things are falling apart. There's trouble right here. And I don't know what to do. At times I feel as if this world is careening out of control. Between terrorist threats, the economy, and the war, there seems to be no peace. But yet when I come to You, I can have peace. Your peace. Speak to me, Lord. Answer me when I call. Help my spirit to rest in You, in this moment and throughout this day.

In the day of my trouble I will call on You, for You will answer me.

PSALM 86:7 AMP

Beaten Down

I think this is the worst day of my life, Lord. I am totally beaten down. I have been pushed around, strung up, held down, kicked out. The influence of the evil one seems to be surrounding me. I can hardly catch my breath. I feel like Elijah. I have had enough, Lord! Help me! The only thing getting me through this is coming into Your presence, remembering that You are by my side through it all. Thank You, Lord, for going through this with me. Help me to focus on You and not on my circumstances. Help me to live in You.

We've been surrounded and battered by troubles, but we're not demoralized;
we're not sure what to do, but we know that God knows what to do;
we've been spiritually terrorized, but God hasn't left our side;
we've been thrown down, but we haven't broken.

2 Corinthians 4:8–9 MSG

Blessings amid the Storm

Lord, when I look back on all the ways You have blessed me and continue to bless me, even through these trials, I am awed and thankful. As You have delivered me in the past, deliver me again from the troubles before me. Lift the burdens off my sagging shoulders. I leave them at the foot of Your cross, as instructed. Thank You, Lord. I love You so much. Now with each breath I take, I relax and enter into Your rest.

I said to myself, "Relax and rest. God has showered you with blessings."

PSALM 116:7 MSG

Flying Away to Safety

My heart is so heavy it hurts. Lift the burden from me, Lord. Take away these feelings of fear. All I want to do is run away, fly out of here. I lift my soul unto You, Lord, seeking Your face, Your peace, Your rest. I call out to You, Lord. "Save me! Lift me! Take me into Your presence!" With each cry of my heart and tear from my eye, I come closer to You, where I am safe, where nothing can harm me, where I can be at peace.

My heart is grievously pained within me. . . . Fear and trembling have come upon me; horror and fright have overwhelmed me. And I say, Oh, that I had wings like a dove! I would fly away and be at rest. . . . I will call upon God, and the Lord will save me.

Psalm 55:4, 5–6, 16 AMP

The Secret Joy in Jesus

I come to You today, meeting You in that secret place where I know I am safe. You are my Rock, my Sure Foundation. Hiding in You, I will come to no harm. I rest in this place, seeking Your face. Jesus, Jesus, Jesus. There is magic in that name. There is peace in this place. There is love in Your eyes. I praise Your holy name! I smile in Your presence. You are the joy of my life!

He who dwells in the secret place of the Most High shall remain stable and fixed under the shadow of the Almighty [Whose power no foe can withstand].

Psalm 91:1 AMP

The Power of Unity

Now the multitude of those who believed were of one heart and one soul. . . . And with great power the apostles gave witness to the resurrection of the Lord Jesus. And great grace was upon them all.

Acts 4:32–33 NKJV

The ultimate power of prayer is found in a church where people of one mind unite. In the Old Testament, God decreed that "mine house shall be called an house of prayer for all people" (Isaiah 56:7 KJV), and in the New Testament Jesus tells us that "where two or three are gathered together in my name, there am I in the midst of them" (Matthew 18:20 KJV). God's decree, Jesus' promised presence, and our unity of mind combine to create one of the most powerful forces on earth—a united, praying church!

When Jesus taught us how to pray, He didn't begin with "*My* Father which art in heaven" but "*Our* Father which art in heaven." He continued: "Give *us* this day *our* daily bread. And forgive *us our* debts, as *we* forgive *our* debtors. And lead *us* not into temptation, but deliver *us* from evil" (Matthew 6:9, 11–12 KJV, emphasis added). Through this one lesson, could the Son of God have made it any clearer that prayer was to be a corporate effort of united minds?

The evidence of the power of unity, of gathering together and praying in one accord, is staggering! And it's not only the *power* felt amid Christ's presence, but the *joy*—the gladness and singleness of heart—of a holy fellowship!

The church is the place where we are all reminded of the power of unity under God. It is where our focus is to be solely on the heavens above, a place where we gather with one common purpose—to love God and each other. In such a spiritual haven, in the midst of Christ's presence, fellow believers are pulled away from earthly concerns and look to Christ seated in the heavenlies with God. There is no greater joy!

Edifying Others

Lord, I will be meeting with others at church today. I want to be an encourager of Your servants, stimulating others, drawing them closer to You. Plant a good word in my heart, one I can use to edify others. Point out a verse from my Bible reading today that someone else needs to hear. Give me the right moment, the right words. And if it's a listening ear someone needs, give me the wisdom of silence. Lead me to do Your will this day.

Let us consider how to stimulate one another to love and good deeds, not forsaking our own assembling together, as is the habit of some, but encouraging one another.

HEBREWS 10:24–25 NASB

Unceasing Prayer

God, I remember how Peter's friends prayed for him while he was in prison, how they constantly and consistently interceded for him. You sent an angel to visit Peter and his chains fell off! Help me to be such a prayer warrior today. Lord, tell me whom to pray for this morning. And may such deliverance come to that person according to Your will.

Prayer was made without ceasing of the church unto God for him.

Acts 12:5 KJV

Jesus in Our Midst

Lord, it's so amazing that when we come together with other believers—even when just two believers are together—You show up! You are in the midst of us! You love us that much. Be with Your body of believers today, Lord, whenever and wherever they are meeting around the world. Show them Your power, Your presence. Answer their prayers today, Lord. All to Your glory!

For where two or three are gathered together in my name,
there am I in the midst of them.

MATTHEW 18:20 KJV

Testimony of Believers

Lord, when I hear what other people say You have done in their lives, their testimonies buoy my own faith. It gives me chills when I hear of the wonders of Your deeds. Give me the courage to share my testimony with others, knowing this will draw unbelievers to You and strengthen the hearts of those who already know You. Thank You, Lord, for hearing my prayer.

They were heartily welcomed by the church and the apostles and the elders, and they told them all that God had accomplished through them.

ACTS 15:4 AMP

Missions

I don't know if I could serve in a foreign country, Lord, but there are others who will and do. God bless them. Give them strength and protection in these perilous days. Speak to their hearts. Specifically I pray for [your church's missionaries' names]. Make their message clear. Aid them in their journey. Open the hearts of those around them who dwell in darkness. Spread Your light among the nations, O God.

Then it seemed good to the apostles and the elders, with the whole church, to choose men from among them and send them to Antioch.

Acts 15:22 ESV

One Body

When one of us is suffering, Lord, we all hurt. Some of my church are grieving, some are burned out, some are of ill health and unsound mind, and some are in financial distress. Lord, bless the people who make up the body of my church. Give them love and comfort. Make this body a unified body, strengthened by Your Spirit and Your love, gathered to meet in Your presence, formed to do Your will.

We are members one of another.

EPHESIANS 4:25 KJV

Singing Praise

All I want to do in church is sing, Lord. I don't care what kind of music it is—contemporary or traditional—as long as it edifies You. All I know is that I want to be with fellow believers and in Your presence. Give me amazing grace to stand with my fellow believers in the midst of the church and sing praises unto You. Thank You for the joy of music, Lord!

Saying, I will declare thy name unto my brethren, in the midst of the church will I sing praise unto thee.

HEBREWS 2:12 KJV

Church Division

Lord, how can those who are united in belief be so divided in other areas? Please, God, You know what is causing strife in Your house of prayer. Please soothe it with Your healing balm. Give our leaders and members wisdom. Pour out upon us Your love and remind us of the love we have for each other. Heal the breach, Lord. I put all these concerns in Your hands. Give me the wisdom to leave them there.

When you come together as a church, I hear that divisions exist among you.

1 Corinthians 11:18 NASB

Edify the Church

Lord, I'm eager to serve You, but I'm not really sure what my gift is. And I don't want to make a fool of myself by trying something and having it be a flop. Give me guidance as to where, when, and how You want me to serve. Give me a gift that will build up Your church. Speak to me clearly as I go throughout this day and the days to come. And if there ever does come a time when You want me to bow out of a ministry, give me the wisdom to do so.

Since you are eager for gifts of the Spirit,
try to excel in those that build up the church.
1 Corinthians 14:12 NIV

Foundation of Truth

There is no stronger foundation than that of Your truth, which is what our church is built upon. We are not a church made up of stone, stucco, brick, or wood but of people from all walks of life. We are a church of the Living God. Oh, what a glorious thing! Make our church strong, Lord, so that we can shine Your light into our community, state, and world!

The church of the living God is the strong foundation of truth.

1 Timothy 3:15 CEV

Fellowship

When we gather together in Your house, we not only have fellowship with each other, but we meet with You, Your Son, and Your Spirit. Breathe on us, Lord. Allow us to unite in prayer and feel Your presence among us. Lead us to the font of eternal blessing and give us strength to do Your will and wisdom to apply Your Word. Increase our body as You did with the early church in the beginning of the book of Acts. We want to see new believers come to experience Your peace and Your love!

That which we have seen and heard we proclaim also to you, so that you too may have fellowship with us; and indeed our fellowship is with the Father and with his Son Jesus Christ.

1 John 1:3 ESV

The Power of Commitment

Commit your work to the Lord, and your plans will be established.
Proverbs 16:3 NRSV

God the Potter has created each of us for a specific purpose and continually shapes us as it seems good to Him (see Jeremiah 18:4). For what has God fashioned you? If you're not sure, pray for guidance, with a mind open enough to accept whatever the Lord tells you. Romans 12:2 says, "Let God. . .give you a new mind. Then you will know what God wants you to do" (NLV). Such seeking is an ongoing process. God's direction must persistently be petitioned since today's work may merely be the training ground for the job He has planned but we have yet to discover.

Once you have prayed and heard God's direction, have the courage to walk where He leads, remembering that He will always go before you (see Isaiah 52:12). Don't let fear give you lead feet. Instead, rest in the assurance that God will "give you every good thing you need so you can do what He wants" (Hebrews 13:21 NLV). God will give you courage, gifts, and opportunities, as well as combine your experience, talents, and knowledge, in order to place you where He needs you. Each day tap into the power of commitment, keeping your course steady so that you will be amply rewarded, now and at the end of your journey, as a "good and faithful servant" (Matthew 25:23 NLV).

Daily commit your work to God and consistently seek His direction. Remember that He continually opens doors for His children (see 1 Corinthians 16:9; 2 Corinthians 2:12; and Colossians 4:3)—but keep your ears open to His voice and your eyes open to opportunity.

Guided by the Spirit

I understand, Lord, that the Holy Spirit is just waiting to lead me. Open my mind and heart and ears to His voice today. Still the constant chatter in my head that keeps reminding me of all the tasks I need to get done today. Give me the plan You have already laid out for my life. Shape me into the person You want me to be so that I can do what You have created me to do. Lead me step by step, Lord. I commit my way and my plans to Your purpose.

Let the Holy Spirit lead you in each step. . . .
If the Holy Spirit is living in us, let us be led by Him in all things.
GALATIANS 5:16, 25 NLV

My Purpose

Lord, what am I supposed to do? I'm not sure why I'm at this job. Or am I not to have a career but be a stay-at-home parent? Have I made the wrong decision? Am I walking in Your will, or have I been led by my own desires? Show me, Lord, which way You want me to go. If there is some new challenge You want me to undertake, please tell me. Let me hear Your voice. Renew my mind this morning so that I can know Your good and perfect will for my life.

The Lord has made everything for its purpose.

Proverbs 16:4 NRSV

Spirit-Filled

You have filled me with Your Spirit. I have been given wisdom, understanding, education, and talent for many lines of work. Show me how I can use my knowledge, understanding, and abilities to do the work You have set out for me. Show me the paths You want me to take. What do You want me to do with my hands, my life, my gifts? They are all from You, the One I want to serve.

"I have filled him with the Spirit of God in wisdom, understanding, much learning, and all kinds of special work."

EXODUS 31:3 NLV

A New Mind

I'm so confused, Lord. I seem to have the wrong mindset today. Instead of looking to Your leading, I seem to be focused in on the worldly aspects of life. And I know that's not where You want my thoughts to be. Give me the mind of Christ. Make my needs simple. Change my life, my thoughts, my desires. I want to live a life that is good, perfect, and pleasing to You.

Let God change your life. First of all, let Him give you a new mind. Then you will know what God wants you to do. And the things you do will be good and pleasing and perfect.

ROMANS 12:2 NLV

The Right God

Lord, I don't want to live my life working for money, power, possessions, position, or status. I want to live for You, work for You, be with You. Keep Yourself in the forefront of my mind this morning and throughout this day. You are the One I worship and the One I serve. You and no one else. Live through me this day. Give me joy in the journey. Lead me to the source of eternal blessing. Thank You, Lord, for saving my soul for Your use!

"If you ever forget the Lord your God and go to other gods to worship and work for them, I tell you today that you will be destroyed for sure."
DEUTERONOMY 8:19 NLV

God Gives the Power

You are the One who has brought me to where I am today. Thank You, God, for giving me power and strength. All the blessings I have in this life come from Your hand. Continue to lead me in Your way. My ears desperately seek to hear Your voice. My heart longs for Your presence. Although I may not be rich in a worldly sense, I am rich in my love of You. Further my knowledge and increase my talents so that I can do the work You desire.

"Be careful not to say in your heart, 'My power and strong hand have made me rich.' But remember the Lord your God. For it is He Who is giving you power to become rich."

DEUTERONOMY 8:17–18 NLV

A Place for My Gifts

Lord, I'm not currently using the gifts I believe You gave me. Help me find a place where I can use my talents, experience, and knowledge to Your good. And while I am in my current position, help me to do my work for Your glory, because You are the manager of my life. Give me Your peace, joy, and direction. I so desperately need to spend these moments in Your presence to prepare my spirit for the tasks of this day. Do not leave me, Lord. Stay in my heart now and forever.

Be sure to use the gift God gave you.

1 TIMOTHY 4:14 NLV

Working to His Honor

Everything I do and everything I have is for Your honor and Your glory—not mine! I am the ambassador of Your one and only Son, Jesus Christ. Give me that attitude today, so that everyone who looks at me, hears me, and speaks to me will see His face and feel His presence. I want to become less so that He can become more. I am Your servant, Lord—help me to serve productively and creatively. All, Lord, to Your honor!

Do everything to honor God.

1 Corinthians 10:31 NLV

Needful and Good

Lord, I want to do what You want me to do. In order to accomplish that, there are a few things I need—Your gifting, direction, strength, and power. Fill me with these things as I commit my life, my work, my day to You. And at the end of the day and the end of my life, may You say to me, "Well done, good and faithful servant!" And may Christ have all the glory. Lord, let it be so!

May God give you every good thing you need so you can do what He wants. . . .
May Christ have all the shining-greatness forever! Let it be so.
HEBREWS 13:21 NLV

The Right Attitude

I'm getting tired of my job and my boss, Lord. It seems like the same thing day in and day out. I know I should be grateful for the work I have been given, but I can't seem to get past this wall of negativity. Give me the right mindset, Lord, before I even go into work. And then help me remember that I am working for You. Give me the mind and servant attitude of Christ this morning and help me maintain it throughout this day.

Be glad you can do the things you should be doing. Do all things without arguing and talking about how you wish you did not have to do them.

PHILIPPIANS 2:14 NLV

His Work Plan

My goal is to live the life You have planned for me. Keep me on the road to Your will. Show me the ways You want me to go. Help me avoid the worldly traps of money, discontentment, grief, envy, workaholism, and tedium. Keep me close to Your side and consistently in Your presence, ever open to hearing Your voice. Give me the power to live Your plan for me. Thank You for all You are doing in my life!

We will follow the plan of the work He has given us to do.

2 Corinthians 10:13 NLV

The Power of Forgiveness

"And when you stand praying, if you hold anything against anyone, forgive them, so that your Father in heaven may forgive you your sins."
MARK 11:25 NIV

Forgiving those who offend us is difficult at best. The more heinous the infraction, the harder it is to pardon the perpetrator. Yet that is exactly what Jesus calls us to do. It amazes me how family squabbles can keep siblings and other family members from talking to each other for the rest of their lives—or how one careless word from a friend can sever a lifelong relationship.

But if we know there is such freedom in forgiveness, why does it seem so hard? We must ask ourselves, "If Jesus can be stripped naked, beaten, scourged, have nails driven into his hands and feet, hang on a cross until death, and still say, 'Father, forgive them for they know what not they do' (see Luke 23:34), why can't we?" "Oh well," you say, "it was easy for Him. He was God." Yet God insists we forgive others no matter how big or small the offenses. But how do we tap into His power of forgiveness?

The first step is to allow yourself to feel the hurt of the offenses against you, both past and present. Pray for the release of that hurt, and then pray for the power to forgive as God constantly and consistently forgives you. Continue to pray until you have truly forgiven in your heart. (It may not happen immediately, but it *will* happen.) Then thank God for His goodness and peace. Finally, when the time is right, try to restore your relationship with the person who hurt you. Pray for the right words to say. All the while, keep in mind that, although your offender's behavior may not change, you will, becoming more like Christ!

Don't poison yourself with the bitter pill of *unforgiveness*—it's suicide! Instead, tap into the power of *forgiveness*, keeping Jesus' peace in mind, His mercy in your heart, His power at hand, and your relationships whole.

Two-Way Forgiveness

It's a two-way street, Lord—we forgive others and then You will forgive us. I know I've read that scripture a hundred times, but I've never understood it more fully than today. Give me the strength of Your forgiveness this morning, Lord. Help me to love and not hate the person who has hurt me. Thank You for releasing the poison of unforgiveness that has been building up within me.

"And when you stand praying, if you hold anything against anyone, forgive them, so that your Father in heaven may forgive you your sins."

MARK 11:25 NIV

Forgiving My Friend

I've about had it, Lord. I don't know how much more of this I can take! Is this friendship even worth all this pain? Lord, please calm me down. Give me the right attitude. Your Word says that no matter how many times I am offended, if my friend apologizes and says she'll never do it again, I am to forgive her. Well, You're going to have to give me this power, because I have none left of my own. Please work, live, and love through me. Help me to forgive my friend.

"Be alert. If you see your friend going wrong, correct him. If he responds, forgive him. Even if it's personal against you and repeated seven times through the day, and seven times he says, 'I'm sorry, I won't do it again,' forgive him."

Luke 17:3–4 MSG

Easily Offended

Lord, I have such anger within me for all the wrongs done me all day long. Even when I'm out in traffic and someone cuts me off, I'm really miffed. Or when my family comes to the dinner table and no one appreciates how hard I've worked to make this meal but complains about every little thing, I just want to scream! Give me that new heart. Empty this heart of stone, the one so easily offended. Fill it with Your love.

"I will give you a new heart and put a new spirit within you. I will take away your heart of stone and give you a heart of flesh."

EZEKIEL 36:26 NLV

No Guilt Trips, Please

I don't know why, Lord, but I just keep bringing up old offenses and throwing them into the faces of those who have hurt me. I know that's not how You want me to behave. If I keep on this course, there's no telling how many people I will alienate from my life. And I'm not being a very good example of a Christian. Help me to forgive others and not remind them of past misdeeds. Help me to pour out Your love to all.

Now is the time to forgive this man and help him back on his feet.
If all you do is pour on the guilt, you could very well drown him in it.
My counsel now is to pour on the love.

2 Corinthians 2:7–8 MSG

Spreading Forgiveness

Lord, when Peter denied You three times, he wept bitterly. I know just how he felt. But You knew that's what he was going to do, and You gave him words to keep him from wallowing in self-pity. You told Peter to strengthen his brethren after he turned back to You. So, I come before You this morning, asking You to forgive me and help me to forgive myself. Then, Lord, give me the opportunity to strengthen others who are dealing with unforgiveness. Help me encourage them to reconcile with those who they have hurt or who have hurt them. All for Your glory, Lord.

[Jesus said,] *"When you have returned to Me, strengthen your brethren."*

LUKE 22:32 NKJV

Needing Mercy

Lord, I am so mad at myself. I have been doing wrong and hiding it from everyone. I even imagined I could hide it from You, but You know all. Lord, please forgive me for not admitting my sins to You. Help me to do better. I don't want to live this way. Sometimes I can't stand myself. Please help me to turn from this behavior. Give me Your never-ending mercy and eternal loving-kindness.

People who conceal their sins will not prosper,
but if they confess and turn from them, they will receive mercy.
PROVERBS 28:13 NLT

Forgive Me!

God, I've messed up again. I can hardly forgive myself. But when my foot slips, Your mercy holds me up! Forgive my offenses, Lord. Take away this feeling of anxiety within me. Help me to stop belittling and berating myself. My confidence is so low. Comfort my soul with Your presence, Your love, Your Spirit. And as You keep forgiving me, help me to forgive others.

If I say, "My foot slips," Your mercy, O Lord, will hold me up.
In the multitude of my anxieties within me, Your comforts delight my soul.

Psalm 94:18–19 NKJV

Forgive and Forget

Why can't I forgive and forget, Lord? Please help me forgive the person who injured me the other day. Instill in me Your power, Your grace, and Your mercy. With each breath I take in Your presence, I feel that power growing within me. Thank You, Lord. Now, please give me the means to forget this pain. I don't want to keep bringing it up and picking at the wound. Help me, Lord, as weak as I am, to forgive the offender and forget the pain.

"Their sins and their lawless deeds I will remember no more."

HEBREWS 10:17 NASB

No Room for the Evil One

When I can't forgive, when I can't control my anger, I know I am giving the devil a foothold into my relationships and situations. And that is not a good thing. Help me to be a forgiving person, looking for healing and reconciliation instead of bitterness and retribution. You are my life and my light. Forgive me for my attitude last night and give me Your love and power today.

When angry, do not sin; do not ever let your wrath (your exasperation, your fury or indignation) last until the sun goes down. Leave no [such] room or foothold for the devil [give no opportunity to him].

EPHESIANS 4:26–27 AMP

My Past Offenses

When I look at my past, at the things I have done, I feel so unworthy of Your forgiveness, Lord. I can't even forgive myself. Please take pity upon me. Forgive me for all my past misdeeds. Give me a clean slate, beginning with this morning. Plant Your Word in my heart. Help me to forgive myself, as this guilt is eating away at my heart. You forgive our sins as far as the east is from the west. Thank You, God, for your mercy! Take my sins, forgive them, and make me whiter than snow in Your eyes.

Keep up your reputation, God; forgive my bad life; it's been a very bad life.

Psalm 25:11 MSG

Quick Forgiveness

You have chosen me to be Your child. Help me to live that life dressed in Your love. I need Your kindness, humility, quiet strength, discipline, and definitely Your even temper. Help me to forgive others as quickly as You forgive us. Do not let bitterness rot my soul. Thank You for the gift of forgiveness. Adorn me with Your love today and every day!

So, chosen by God for this new life of love, dress in the wardrobe God picked out for you: compassion, kindness, humility, quiet strength, discipline. Be even-tempered, content with second place, quick to forgive an offense. Forgive as quickly and completely as the Master forgave you. And regardless of what else you put on, wear love. It's your basic, all-purpose garment. Never be without it.

COLOSSIANS 3:12–14 MSG

The Power of Love

Let's not merely say that we love each other;
let us show the truth by our actions.
1 John 3:18 NLT

When you and your spouse said, "I do," you promised to love, honor, and cherish each other "until death do [you] part." That's quite a vow of commitment to make before family, friends, and God. And it is one you are meant to keep. The power of staunch commitment is an awesome thing when combined with the power of love.

Once committed, you need to communicate. Don't become so caught up in the world that you become two ships passing in the night, merely blaring your horns once in a while and then heading into separate seas. And when you do converse, watch your words and also *mean* what you say.

Now that you're communicating, take the time to compliment each other. As the years progress, husbands and wives tend to get into a rut. Prevent your rut from becoming a chasm by "rejoic[ing] in the wife [or husband] of your youth" (Proverbs 5:18 NIV). When you work at praising and complimenting each other day after day, the flame of your love will burn ever greater and you'll find yourselves rejoicing in each other's presence.

But commitment, communication, and compliments will be hollow at best unless you care for each other using the power of the *love* described in 1 Corinthians 13:4–8. Make it a point to practice this love every day.

Pray for each other and fuel your marriage with the power of love so that you may "enjoy life with the [one] whom you love all the days of your fleeting life. . .for this is your reward" (Ecclesiastes 9:9 NASB). And at night when the lights go out, take time to adore that special person God has made just for you.

Two in One

Lord, my spouse and I are two who have been united into one. I praise You and thank You for leading me to my other half. He is more than I could ever have hoped for or dreamed. Bless our marriage, bless our union, bless our lives. Help us to grow closer together with each passing year. Lead us to do what You have called us to do, as one standing before You this day.

" 'A man will leave his father and mother and be united to his wife, and the two will become one flesh.' . . . So they are no longer two, but one flesh. Therefore what God has joined together, let no one separate."

MATTHEW 19:5–6 NIV

My Reward in Life

Life passes so quickly, Lord. Yet for this precious amount of time I have here on earth, I want to enjoy life with my spouse. He/she is so dear to me. Thank You for rewarding me with his presence in the morning as I wake and at night when the lights go out. Thank You for filling me with thoughts of my lover throughout the day. Bless my spouse this morning. Let Your love flow through me and into my other half.

Enjoy life with the [one] *whom you love all the days of your fleeting life which He has given to you under the sun; for this is your reward in life.*

Ecclesiastes 9:9 NASB

Stronger Every Day

Lord, my spouse and I have been through such trials, yet each time we make it over a hurdle together, our love grows stronger. What we had in the beginning of our marriage was good, but what we have now is better. Continue to help us through the trials of this life. Help us to keep a united front before our children. And in all things, may we praise Your name for the wonders and joy of marital love.

For if what is passing away was glorious, what remains is much more glorious.

2 Corinthians 3:11 NKJV

Wounded and Bleeding

Lord, help us to put our past troubles behind us and look forward to the days ahead. Help us to forget some of the things that we have done and said to each other. Our marriage is wounded and bleeding, Lord. We need Your balm of love to heal it. Give us Your special touch so that we may never part. For what You have brought together shall not be put asunder. Give us strength, hope, wisdom, and guidance.

This one thing I do, forgetting those things which are behind, and reaching forth unto those things which are before.

PHILIPPIANS 3:13 KJV

Choosing Words Carefully

I did it again, Lord. I spoke before I thought and now I have wounded my spouse. According to Your Word, there is more hope for a fool than for me. I feel so terrible about what I said. I know I cannot take away the words I have spoken. All I can say is that I'm sorry. Forgive me, Father, for the words I spoke. My heart is so heavy within me. Give me the courage to ask my spouse for forgiveness. And may this rift in our union be speedily mended. Heal our marriage, Lord. Give me hope.

Do you see a man who is quick with his words?
There is more hope for a fool than for him.
Proverbs 29:20 NLV

Anger Issues

I did it again, Lord. I went to bed angry with my spouse and spent a sleepless night because of it. I feel awful today. My spouse and I went our separate ways this morning with tension between us. Now we'll be brooding about it all day. Calm my anger, Lord. Forgive me for letting it go this long. Give us the right words to say to each other when we are alone again tonight. Help us heal this breach, to Your glory.

If you are angry, do not let it become sin.
Get over your anger before the day is finished.
EPHESIANS 4:26 NLV

Undying Love

My love for my spouse will never die, Lord, because we believe in You. We know You have brought us together and will keep us together. We will never give up on this marriage, nor lose faith in each other, nor lose hope in our circumstances. We are in this until the end and, although we may not love every minute of it, we do love each other and You. And because of that, we are growing stronger every day. Thank You, Jesus, for the power of love!

Love never gives up, never loses faith,
is always hopeful, and endures through every circumstance.
1 CORINTHIANS 13:7 NLT

The Power of Words

Everyone should be quick to listen, slow to speak and slow to become angry.
James 1:19 niv

Words have power. We can use words to heal or harm, lift or lower, teach or taunt. When you talk to your spouse, children, and parents, are your words building them up or tearing them down? Have you said things that you wished you could take back?

Our children are what they eat. What words are you feeding your family? Words poisoned with sarcasm, tainted with anger, and seasoned with insults? Or nourishing morsels laced with praise, colored with encouragement, and spiced with honor?

What steps can you take to ensure that you are feeding your family, your children, a healthy conversational diet? First, when communicating, *be quick to listen.*

Second, be *slow to speak*. Think and pray before you let any words come out of your mouth. Proverbs 16:1 says, "The plans of the mind and orderly thinking belong to man, but from the Lord comes the [wise] answer of the tongue" (Proverbs 16:1 amp). Praying *before* speaking will save you a lot of heartache.

When you do speak, be *slow to become angry*. Keep a rein on your emotions by using "patient persistence [which] pierces through indifference; gentle speech [which] breaks down rigid defenses" (Proverbs 25:15 the message).

Ask God to help you gain control of your tongue. Use your words to build up your family members (see 1 Thessalonians 5:11). Honor others—those above (parents, grandparents), beside (spouses), and below you (children and grandchildren)—more than you honor yourself (see Philippians 2:3), by listening to them, praying before you speak, and responding in gentleness.

Morning Prayer

Lord, here I am this morning, awaiting Your words of wisdom. I need to have a talk with my child today and I don't know what to say or how to say it. Give me direction. Open my eyes, heart, and spirit to understanding Your will for me and my child. I want to know how to speak words to comfort, direct, and assist him/her. Help me, O Lord. Guide the words of my tongue.

The Sovereign Lord has given me his words of wisdom, so that I know how to comfort the weary. Morning by morning he wakens me and opens my understanding to his will.

Isaiah 50:4 NLT

Made a Mistake

O God, if only I could control my tongue! My life is more like "Open mouth, insert foot." And that's just what I've done. Is there any way to remedy this situation? Help me in this endeavor. Give me the courage to be humble, to go to my child and admit I've made a mistake. May he/she forgive me as I have forgiven my child so often in the past, and how You constantly forgive all of us. Help us put this incident behind us. Give me the wisdom to do better next time. All to Your glory!

Indeed, we all make many mistakes. For if we could control our tongues, we would be perfect and could also control ourselves in every other way.

JAMES 3:2 NLT

Curb My Tongue

Lord, my tongue just went on and on—and now I am reaping the consequences. When will I ever learn when to stop talking? It seems I continually belabor a point until my child has zoned out and becomes unresponsive. Help me to weigh my words carefully, to say only what You want me to say. In other words, help me to zip up my mouth!

The tongue can bring death or life;
those who love to talk will reap the consequences.
PROVERBS 18:21 NLT

Jesus' Word Power

I try and try, but my efforts accomplish nothing when I have not come first to You in prayer. I need to do things in Your strength for otherwise I am useless. I need Your power behind me when I speak. I need Your strength. Allow Your Word to speak to me. Guide my way by Your gentle voice. May my spirit and Yours become one this day.

[Jesus said,] *"The Spirit alone gives eternal life. Human effort accomplishes nothing. And the very words I have spoken to you are spirit and life."*

JOHN 6:63 NLT

Honoring Others

I don't need fancy words to impress others. I only need words guided by the mind of Christ. Help me, Lord, to honor others with my speech. I want to lift people up, not bring them down. I want to bring joy to the hearts of others. Give me a better attitude, positive words, and encouraging remarks. Guard my mouth and, when necessary, put Your hand upon it to keep it shut.

Don't try to impress others.
Be humble, thinking of others as better than yourselves.
PHILIPPIANS 2:3 NLT

Kind versus Cutting Words

Words have cut me to the quick. Now I know how others feel when I harm them with my words. It really hurts. I feel very wounded. My stomach is filled with anger, sorrow, embarrassment, bitterness, and rage. Lord, give me a kind thought from Your Word today, scripture that will heal and build me back up. Take this sorrow from me and replace it with a spirit of forgiveness. Lift me up to Your rock of refuge.

Kind words heal and help; cutting words wound and maim.

PROVERBS 15:4 MSG

Building Up

Okay, Lord, today not one negative thought is going to go through my head and come of out my mouth. This morning I will drench myself in Your Word and come out smiling. I want to spread to others the joy You plant in my heart. Give me the right words to say at the right moment to build up others. Give me words of praise, words of wisdom, and words of encouragement.

Encourage (admonish, exhort) one another and edify (strengthen and build up) one another.

1 Thessalonians 5:11 AMP

Living My Faith

Lord, I want to live my faith before my children and others. To do that I need to be able to control my words, but sometimes, although I know this is impossible, my tongue seems to have a "mind" of its own. Help me rein in my mouth. Give me words that will lead my children to You. Help me to live a life that is rich in Your love—and may that love affect my speech. Begin with me this morning and show me how to live this faith.

If you claim to be religious but don't control your tongue, you are fooling yourself, and your religion is worthless.

JAMES 1:26 NLT

Needing a Tender Heart

Take away all the bitterness I feel today, and with it the anger and words I want to say but know I shouldn't. Help me not to avenge my honor with evil words. Give me Your tender heart. Help me to forgive the one who has hurt me, just as You, Lord, forgave me. Make this a new morning. Wipe the slate clean. I want to live as You did, Lord, with gentle words, a peaceful spirit, and a loving heart.

Let all bitterness, wrath, anger, clamor, and evil speaking be put away from you, with all malice. And be kind to one another, tenderhearted, forgiving one another, even as God in Christ forgave you.

EPHESIANS 4:31–32 NKJV

The Power of Faith-Based Boldness

When we trust in him, we're free to say whatever needs to be said, bold to go wherever we need to go.
Ephesians 3:11 MSG

When David left his father's fields to check on his brothers who were with King Saul's army, it was not by chance that his visit coincided with the nine-foot-nine-inch-tall Philistine warrior named Goliath, who was defying the army of Israel. As David began talking to the soldiers, he encountered his first challenge in the form of his oldest brother Eliab, who said: "Why have you come down? And with whom have you left those few sheep in the wilderness? I know your insolence and the wickedness of your heart; for you have come down in order to see the battle" (1 Samuel 17:28 NASB).

David's next confrontation was with King Saul, who "from his shoulders upward. . .was taller than any of the [other children of Israel]" (1 Samuel 9:2 NKJV). Now, you'd think that because of his size Saul himself would have fought Goliath. Instead, Saul tried to discourage the only one willing to face the giant. Saul said to David: "There's no way you can fight this Philistine and possibly win! You're only a boy, and he's been a man of war since his youth" (1 Samuel 17:33 NLT).

David had always relied on God to deliver him and he wasn't about to stop doing so now—nor was he going to allow Saul to dampen his enthusiasm. Because of his intimate knowledge of God, David was able to turn away from a maligner, defend himself before a discourager, and fell a giant intimidator with one smooth stone. By using faith-based boldness, David met the challenges presented to him and, as a result, routed the entire Philistine army. All for God's glory!

If we build up our confidence by spending time in the Word, prayer, and meditation, getting to know our God intimately, we can be like David, who, with faith-based boldness, "rose early in the morning" (1 Samuel 17:20 NKJV) to meet every challenge God put in his path.

Going Forward Bodly

Lord, here I am trying to take on this work and others are trying to intimidate me, telling me there is no way I can meet the challenge You have set before me. But I have faith in You. I know that with You in my life, I can do whatever You call me to do. Help me not to let others dissuade me from my goal. Give me the faith that David sought from You, the kind that does not waver but goes boldly forward.

They were just trying to intimidate us, imagining that they could discourage us and stop the work. So I continued the work with even greater determination.

NEHEMIAH 6:9 NLT

Bold and Diligent

I'm working as hard as I can to meet my challenge. I want to do my best, knowing that You are with me all the way. Help me to be brave. Help me not to panic. Neither fear nor anxiety is of You. I need to focus on You, to build up my faith and my confidence. Help me not to deviate from my course. I am here this morning, ready to listen to Your voice. Lead me, gentle Shepherd, where You want me to go.

"Be bold and diligent. And God be with you as you do your best."

2 Chronicles 19:11 MSG

Facing the Unknown

O Lord, I feel called to take on this new challenge. I can feel the Spirit drawing me into this latest endeavor. But I don't know what's going to happen. Oh, how I sometimes wish I could see into the future. Lord, help me to have confidence, trust, and faith in Your will for my life. Help me to just put one foot in front of the other, to do the next thing, to continue walking in Your way. And when I get there, I will give You all the glory!

"And now, compelled by the Spirit, I am going to Jerusalem, not knowing what will happen to me there."

Acts 20:22 NIV

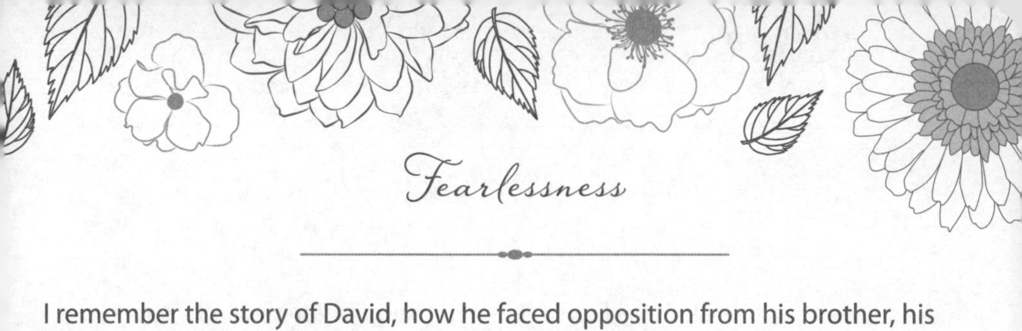

Fearlessness

I remember the story of David, how he faced opposition from his brother, his king, and then a huge giant, all under the watchful eye of his enemies. But he was not afraid. Oh, that I would have such faith. Sometimes I get so scared my heart begins beating a mile a minute. And those are the times when I have taken my eyes off of You. Keep my focus on Your Word. Plant this verse in my heart so that when dread comes upon me, I can say these words and kiss fear good-bye.

Though an army may encamp against me, my heart shall not fear.

Psalm 27:3 NKJV

Standing with God

All of a sudden, I am as alone as David when he stood before Goliath. But I am not going to be mad at others for deserting me. I don't need them. All I need is You. You are my Lord, my Savior, my Deliverer, my Rock, my Refuge. You are by my side. I can feel Your presence right here, right now. Oh, how wonderful You are! Thank You for giving me the power I need. Thank You for never leaving me.

Everyone deserted me. May it not be held against them. But the Lord stood at my side and gave me strength. . . . And I was delivered.

2 Timothy 4:16–17 niv

Support of Fellow Believers

Sometimes those who don't know You think that believers like me are crazy. But we're not. We just know that when You call us to do something, when You put a challenge before us, we are to go forward with no fear. We are bold in You, Lord! How awesome is that! And thankfully, fellow believers encourage us, knowing that if it is Your will, all will be well. What would I do without that support? Thank You for planting my feet in a nice broad place, surrounded by fellow believers who love and pray for me.

When [Paul] *would not be dissuaded, we gave up and said, "The Lord's will be done."*

ACTS 21:14 NIV

Our Help

I need look no further than You, Lord, to help me. It is Your name that I trust. It is Your power that will help me meet this challenge. After all, You made me. You know the plan for my life. You have equipped me to do what You have called me to do. Help me not to rely on myself but on You and Your power. That is what is going to give me victory in this life. Thank You for hearing and answering my prayer.

Our help is in the name of the L*ORD*, *who made heaven and earth.*

PSALM 124:8 NKJV

My Armor

I do not trust in my talents, diligence, money, education, luck, or others to help me meet this challenge. I trust in You. My power is in the faith-based boldness that only comes from knowing You intimately. With that weapon in my arsenal, there is only victory ahead. Those who say I cannot do what You have called me to do will be put to shame. But that's not why I continue to meet this challenge. I go forward because I want to bring glory to You. It is in You that I boast all day long. I praise Your name, my Strength and my Deliverer.

I will not trust in my bow, nor shall my sword save me. But You have saved us from our enemies, and have put to shame those who hated us. In God we boast all day long, and praise Your name forever.

Psalm 44:6–8 NKJV

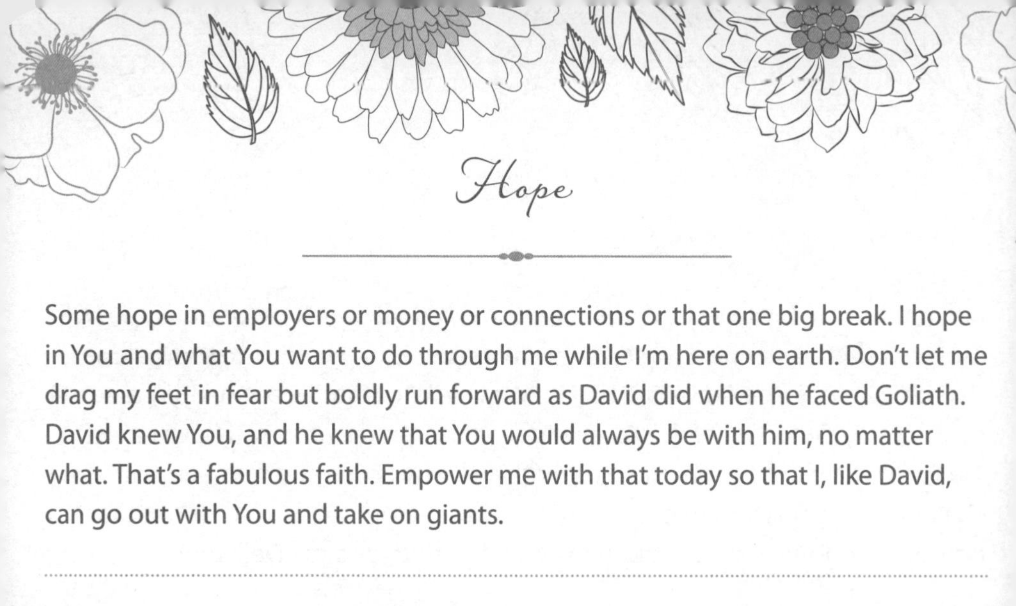

Hope

Some hope in employers or money or connections or that one big break. I hope in You and what You want to do through me while I'm here on earth. Don't let me drag my feet in fear but boldly run forward as David did when he faced Goliath. David knew You, and he knew that You would always be with him, no matter what. That's a fabulous faith. Empower me with that today so that I, like David, can go out with You and take on giants.

"And now, Lord, what do I wait for? My hope is in You."

Psalm 39:7 NKJV

Make Me Bold

Sometimes I feel like a ninety-five-pound weakling when it comes to my faith. I let my doubts and fears overtake me and then find myself shrinking from the challenges You put before me. Lord, I ask You to make me bold. Give me the strength to take on all comers. To do what You want me to do. Dispel the darkness that surrounds me. Bring me to where You want me to be. Give me strength in my soul!

On the day I called, You answered me; You made me bold with strength in my soul.

Psalm 138:3 NASB

By Faith, I Go

In these days of online directional services and personal navigation systems, I can't imagine not knowing where I am going. What Abraham might have given for a map! But that's what faith is all about, isn't it? It's the substance of things hoped for, the evidence of things unseen. Give me that faith, Lord, as I take on this challenge. I don't know where it will lead or how it will all turn out, but by faith I will obey Your call. I will go out, not knowing, because I trust in You!

By faith Abraham, when he was called, obeyed by going out to a place which he was to receive for an inheritance; and he went out, not knowing where he was going.

HEBREWS 11:8 NASB

At the Throne

Here I am again, Lord, coming boldly before You, kneeling at the foot of Your throne. I need Your mercy this morning, and although it seems like I ask for this over and over again, give me more faith, Lord. Help me not to run from this challenge. Give me the grace, strength, energy, talent, and intelligence that I need to make this come out right. I come to You, bowing down, asking for Your love and power to fill me and to give me the strength I need to accomplish the challenges before me this day.

So let us come boldly to the throne of our gracious God. There we will receive his mercy, and we will find grace to help us when we need it most.

HEBREWS 4:16 NLT

In God's Strength

It's amazing—I can do all things through You! You give me the power! You give me the energy! You give me the ways and the means! As I lie here, in Your presence, I feel all the energy emanating from You. Oh, what a feeling! Give me that strength I need to accomplish the goals You set before me. Plant the words, "I can do all things through God—He strengthens me!" in my heart forever and ever.

I have strength for all things in Christ Who empowers me [I am ready for anything and equal to anything through Him Who infuses inner strength into me; I am self-sufficient in Christ's sufficiency].

PHILIPPIANS 4:13 AMP

Conclusion

Prayer has the power to heal the sick, feed the hungry, protect the endangered, replenish the weary, mend the heart, save the soul, strengthen the spirit, transform a life, and change the world. Prayer makes the impossible possible.

Believe in this power. Bolster your faith by delving into God's Word and examining the records of His people. Every morning when you arise you have the opportunity to come to your Lord and Savior and take hold of the power of prayer. Run to His presence. He is waiting for you to seek His face, to ask Him whatever your heart desires.

Approach your quiet time with an eager, open heart, knowing that prayer is the key to your life in Christ. In the early morning silence, allow the Holy Spirit to lead you to God's kingdom. As you spend time in His presence, growing closer to your Lord and Savior, you will become more like Him, filled with His light and love. Then when you rise from those moments in His presence, you will find yourself radiating His love to those around you.

As you grow in God's grace, may your spirit be so transformed that those you meet will be assured they have experienced a glimpse of Christ.

Notes

1. David Jeremiah, *Prayer: The Great Adventure* (Sisters, Ore.: Multnomah, 1997), 75–76.

2. Andrew Murray, *Andrew Murray on Prayer* (New Kensington, Penn.: Whitaker House, 1998), 357.

3. C. S. Lewis, *The Joyful Christian* (New York: Macmillan Publishing Company, 1977), 210.